RANDWICK

AND

ROUNDABOUT

'The views . . . from the heights of Whiteshill, Randwick, and the district in general, are such as can hardly be excelled for picturesque beauty and variety in any part of the kingdom'

(Paul Hawkins Fisher, 1871)

RANDWICK
AND
ROUNDABOUT

Evelyn Pollard

ALAN SUTTON
1986

ALAN SUTTON PUBLISHING
BRUSWICK ROAD · GLOUCESTER

Copyright © Evelyn Pollard 1986

First Published 1986

British Library Cataloguing in Publication Data
Pollard, Evelyn
Randwick and roundabout.
1. Randwick (Gloucestershire) – Social life
and customs
I. Title
942.4'19   DA690.R1/

ISBN 0-86299-042-4

Printed and bound in Great Britain

CONTENTS

To Jane Crosier, my great-niece – who asked me what it was like in my youth.

FOREWORD

T his little memoir by my mother will not 'set the pages alight', but it may warm the heart or raise a smile. It is largely a tribute to my maternal grandparents John and Ellen Pollard and their relations and friends.

My Pollard forbears spent most of the sixteenth, seventeenth and eighteenth centuries working the family farm at Siddington, near Cirencester, which they probably purchased from funds acquired during the sale of Abbey properties in 1545, after the Dissolution. They were mostly churchwardens, literate, and married into the local clergy and merchant classes, but never rose above the level of yeoman farmers.

By the late 18th century, a succession of large and healthy families had reduced overall prosperity, and from James Pollard, my great, great, great grandfather, downwards, the males were mostly journeymen or craftsmen in the Cirencester/Stroud area. As opposed to my father's family – who were perhaps somewhat more spectacular, if less reliable – my mother's recollections offer an intimate view of 'urban' village life in the Gloucester area from Edwardian times to the depression.

No attempt has been made to camouflage names and activities as life was really quite salutary in those days. Significantly, at the height of Empire, the lifestyle which emerges is not 'romantic/pastoral' but small town 'rational/industrial'. A spartan existence. The gentry manage their estates, the tradesmen trade, and craftsmen 'craft'. They spend little time chasing foxes, golfballs, or footballs.

G.A. WENMAN

ACKNOWLEDGEMENTS

I would like to thank all who have helped me to compile these brief memoirs, especially my sister-in-law Evelyn Pollard, and my brother-in-law Fred Barnett. Fortunately they both possess excellent memories. Also Beata Ashmead of Randwick and Harold Robinson of Slad for supplying many details of the village of Randwick as it was, which I had forgotten.

I am indebted to Mr Mike Gooding of Inprint for prints of Great War material and to Mr Lionel Walrond, Curator of Stroud Museum, for details of the Budding mower. Also to Angela Wootton of the Imperial War Museum, for voluntarily researching the L32 material, and to Mr R.J. Carpenter for the eyewitness account.

Mr W.H. Knight has kindly supplied details of the Rowland Ding aircraft landing, which he witnessed.

The original photographs of Randwick and my family are mostly by Merritt Brothers of Stroud, and my brother, the late Arthur Pollard. For the 'reconstructed' sketches I have to thank my son, and would apologise for any artistic licence on his part.

I would also thank the publishers for their moral support.

PART I

CHILDHOOD

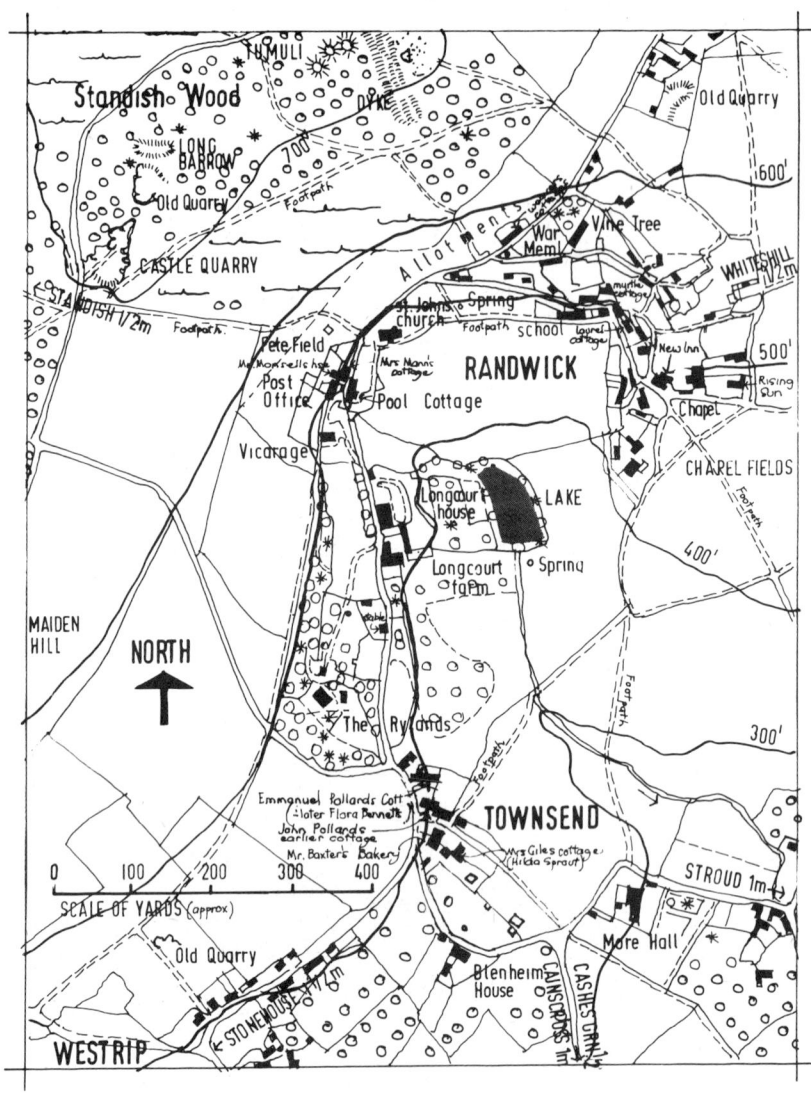

RANDWICK VILLAGE

T his is a photograph of Randwick Old Post Office taken about 1912, where I lived, with occasional absences for vocational reasons, until my marriage in 1925. My younger brother Arthur, and sister Phyllis, are looking out inquisitively from the front porch and old Mrs Manns is proceeding down the hill at left, complete with large straw hat, to chat with cronies at the spring. The vicarage, a rambling Victorian edifice, where resided the Reverend John Hayward, takes up most of the background. The Post Office was the centre of village life and indeed the hub of the universe as far as we kids were concerned.

Randwick Post Office and Vicarage

3

Longcourt

After all, we did possess the only phone in the village – even if it was by
kind permission of the Postmaster General. Rather surprisingly, Nero,
our Manchester terrier, has not managed to get into this photograph, as
I suspect that he had followed my father to work at Fromehall Mill on
this occasion.

The church and C of E school, the fount of all spiritual and temporal
knowledge, was situated conveniently opposite, closely buttressed by
the aristocracy in the respected persons of Colonel and Mrs Anderson at
the Rylands, the Clements at Longcourt, and Mrs Peacock at Pool
Cottage. The rest of the village was disposed above the church – mostly
between the unmetalled tracks leading to the Ash and Whiteshill – as
individual cottages, two up and two down, grouped haphazardly

The Rylands

around pitches or laggards, providing vital arteries for every purpose from coal delivery to social intrigue. This, the village proper, boasted no less than three pubs in those halcyon days; the Vine Tree, still extant, the Rising Sun, adjoining the chapel on the Whiteshill road, and, in between, the New Inn, run by the Mullens family. The latter two are now converted to private dwellings.

The rest of our immediate social community came from Townsend, some half mile below the village on the Cainscross road, or Whiteshill, along the hillside to the north. At this stage of our lives, the rest of the Kingdom, and the Universe, just didn't count! Indeed, in those halcyon days before the 'poverty trap' (largely due, I suspect, to the availability of easy credit), the village constituted an oasis of peace and security only

The Chapel

surpassed by More's Utopia, but attained without external direction. And nowadays the Shell Guide has the gall to describe Randwick as 'an ugly suburb of Stroud'! Why, on Empire Day, after one had been given an orange and a penny and excused school, we *owned* the world.

Randwick is situated at that point of the Cotswold Edge where the River Frome, joined by the Painswick, Slade, and Nailsworth streams, became sufficiently august to break through to the Severn. It is favoured because, though the Edge rises to some 800 feet at this point, it is sheltered from the direct path of the Atlantic Westerlies by that ancient 'barrowed' outcrop known as the Ash, which terminates in Maiden Hill. From the latter, on a fine day, one might obtain superb views to the south-west along the Cotswold escarpment from Rodborough Fort

6

Blenheim House

to Nympsfield, and on to the Severn Estuary, so we were not unaware of the rest of humanity, and the sight of a fleet of trows or luggers sailing up the Severn on the tide, inspired us with all the mystery of the East.

Despite the marked absence of official 'social services' in those days, Randwick was remarkably well provided for. The 'posh' end of the village adjoining the church supplied all the spiritual and intellectual leadership that could be wished, whilst not being in any way oppressive, and at a more practical level, five stalwart individuals provided the essential services. These were Ernie Baxter, Flora Bennett, Bert Harmer, and my parents. There were, of course, others, including the local builder Fred Turner, who was also churchwarden.

Ernie Baxter lived at Townsend and delivered fresh bread daily in his trap drawn by pony Polly. He was renowned for his excellent batch cakes. Flora Bennett, as unofficial district nurse, brought most of the village children into the world, cared for the long-term sick, and laid out the dead. She had an exceptional capacity for hard work, during the performance of which she was boisterously cheerful, except upon sombre occasions, when she exhibited an appropriate sorrow. She was a

7

FLORA BENNETT REASSURES RELATIVES
FOLLOWING A DIFFICULT DELIVERY.

large woman with a heart proportional to her physique; she disdained any social advantage for her good works, and made little pecuniary profit. She now lies buried in the churchyard with most of her progeny.

If Flora was the DHSS, Bert Harmer was the MOT and Bus Company combined, despite his regular work as a small farmer residing at Hill Farm in the village 'upper regions'. He kept a multi-purpose utility vehicle, known locally as Harmer's Hearse, with a single black horse to match. This doubled as wedding car, funeral hearse, and station taxi.

My mother rounded off the public service team by providing the

MY FATHER PUSHED THE HEAVY BARROW ALL THE WAY TO MONE HALL
— AND ALL THE WAY BACK AGAIN — ON APRIL FOOLS DAY.

FROMEHALL MILL AT STROUD WHERE MY FATHER
WORKED AS BLACKSMITH & FETLER 6 DAYS A WEEK

communications centre in the form of the Post Office whilst my father performed the duties of a public works department, besides putting in a six-day week as mill blacksmith and fettler at Fromehall Mill. As the specialised trades of plumber, mechanic and electrical engineer hardly existed locally, he would be called upon to fix anything from a broken cart spring to a privy door. He was indeed so generally helpful that on one occasion when it was reported that the nuns at More Hall were out

10

St John's Church, Randwick, where we spent most of the day on Sunday.

of potatoes, he pushed a heavy barrow-load the half mile journey, only to find that it was April Fool's Day!

Other than the VIP houses and our own cottage, which was purchased on mortgage, I am not sure who owned the property, but the Martin family of Blenheim House at Townsend held a lot and the Roman Church owned the convent of More Hall. Most of the men in the village worked at either the Fromehall or Lodgmore Mills, Dudbridge, or the Brick and Tile Company at Stonehouse and they *walked* there and back.

11

FAMILY

AND

FOREBEARS

My paternal grandfather, Emmanuel Pollard, was born at Leigh, Wiltshire, in 1848, the son of John Pollard, a smallholder. During his training as a journeyman stonemason he met and married Ellen Fletcher at Kings Stanley, Glos. and their first child, Eli Henry, was born in 1866. My father, John James, was born the following year, then Aunts Fanny, Emily and Louise, Uncles Jess and Thomas, and two more Aunts, Ellen and Alice. Surprisingly, all lived, and my father attributed this fertility to the effect of the stone dust!

My great-grandfather, John Pollard of Leigh, was born at Poulton in 1809, the son of James Pollard, who was born at Siddington in 1759. This James was the youngest son of William Pollard and his wife Lydia who held farm lands at Siddington which had been in the family for six generations. William was born in 1713 of John Pollard and his wife Elizabeth, and, in turn, descended from no less than four Williams, the first of whom died in 1606. They were all churchwardens at Siddington St Mary or St Peter, and signed their wills.

I am rather proud that my great, great, great, great, great, great, great, great grandmother, Alice Pollard, sowed her own fields after the death of her husband in 1606, though she herself died several years later. This 'first' William's father is not known for certain, though his mother was Alice Hall of Cirencester, a wool merchant's daughter. However, it seems likely from extant records that he was the son of John Pollard, a civil servant of Henry VIII's court, who was mentioned with one William Byrte in a Parliamentary Roll of 1545 as the joint purchasers of some 152 messuages and tenements at the dissolution of the Abbey. These properties were apparently soon resold, and probably provided the capital to purchase the farm at Siddington.

Of my nine aunts and uncles, Eli Henry died during the Boer War, and Aunt Fanny married Joshua Knight of Berkeley. Aunt Emily married Henry Alder and emigrated to Canada, where they had four

12

Anno dom. (1615) in the fourteenth year of the reign of our Soveraigne L. King James of England and of Scotland ye nine and fourtieth on ye Second day of August.

In ye Counte of Gloucester

In the name of God. Amen. I Alise Pollard widdow of the parish of Syddington Maire in perfect understanding and memore doe institute and ordaine this my last will and testament in manner and form, as followeth. First I commend my soule into the hands of my redeemer and my bodie to be buried in ye church yard of Siddington Maire. Next I give unto my beloved daughter *Christine Pollard* one Cow, besides it which I have formerly given her, half ye acre of barley upon burandino furlong. Next I give unto my sister my biggest brasse pot. Also I give to my daughter *Elnor Pollard* twoo twoo yeare old heyffers, one halfe acre of wheat, *that I sowed my selfe*, my shepe and the little brasse kettels. Also I give to my only sone *William Pollard* one maryage bed on which I lye and all ye furniture, ye cupboard and table in the hall, ye bedsteads, all my wood, milk vessels and [?] within ye house if not prescribed in some part of this my last will and testament. I give unto them all my first part of roane that Walter Hone sowed for me on my land together with ye [?] and hay in the field to be divided by equal portions between them and my executors. Also I appoint my two grounds ye one raked Bidsmoor and the other Clarkpit, and all my summe for the discharge of my rent of the lesing for this year, the residue, if any remayne to be equaly parted amongst them all and my executors. For I appoint these kin for the discharge of my debts. The rest of my goods not given remaining to my eldest daughter *Johan Pollard* (whom I do instate and ordaine my Executor of this my last will and testament), that is to say one Cow, one yearling heyffer, my biggest Calver, and the bed on which she lies, with all ye furniture, half with her sister Christean in ye acre of barley on burandino furlong, the rest of my mares and goats which it is possessed and the half part of ye tything formerly named within this will. Lastly I intreat my beloved friends and neighbours George Spurret, Parson of Siddington Maire, Walter Hone of Siddington, Peter and *Thomas Gegge* the overseers of this my last will and testament.

Wits. George Spurret. Anne Gegge.

Copy of Alice Pollard's Will dated 1615 – by kind permission of Gloucester County Record Office.

Mother, Father, Fred and myself in 1903.

children. Ernest and Leonard returned to Randwick with the Canadian Army during the war and Arthur joined the Canadian Pacific Railway. Ernest became engaged to one of the Whiteshill Bassett girls, but was unfortunately killed in action – and she died shortly afterwards. Leonard returned to Ontario to marry and father Arthur, Ronald and Ruth. Aunt Louise married Walter Dee of Paganhill whilst Uncle Jess served long term with the British Army in Egypt and India, marrying Aunt Jane, a nurse in the Indian Service. He finally retired around 1912 to run a general stores and furniture warehouse at Dursley.

Uncle Tom married Aunt Lucy and went to live at Trowbridge, where he ran an insurance agency and established a smallholding, whilst Uncle William worked as a cellarman at the Cainscross Brewery. Of the younger aunts, Aunt Ellen married Albert Miller and lived at Rodborough, and Aunt Alice married John Young of Carlisle and lived at Gloucester.

My father and mother were both born in 1867, my mother being the daughter of Joseph Birt of Slad, who was also a cellarman at Cainscross Brewery. She was in service at Barton Lodge, Gloucester when she met my father, then a coachbuilder with the Gloucester Carriage and Wagon Company. It was love at first sight, and they were ideally suited. They married at All Saints, Gloucester on the 26th November 1892, and lived initially at 3 Victoria Street. All was not straightforward, however, and their first two sons were stillborn. Much to their joy and relief, my brother Fred was born after they moved to Paganhill in 1898, and survived. I followed in April 1902, after their removal to Townsend, and my brother Arthur in 1904 and sister Phyllis in July 1908. We three were all born in the little end-terrace cottage adjoining my grand-parents' home and which was later to become the abode of Flora Bennett, midwife.

Upon our move to Randwick proper just before the outbreak of the Great War, the family was well established and we felt we had 'arrived' on purchasing our own freehold again. The acquisition of the Post Office licence was also a godsend as it added another few shillings or so to my father's weekly wage of one pound.

CHURCH, SCHOOL
AND
VICARAGE

The church and school at Randwick being solidly 'C of E' and strongly supported by the whole village, we children experienced little of an extreme mystical nature, but plenty of healthy moral virtue. We felt rather sorry for Dick Mullins who, being a catholic, did not attend morning prayers at school. We were, frankly, rather sceptical regarding tales of ghosts seen at More Hall, but nevertheless had a sneaking admiration for Oliver Edmonds, his sisters Kate and Daisy, and Florrie Browning, who walked some two miles daily through the dark recesses of Standish wood from Cherry Fair.

This is not to say that there was not a certain amount of popular superstition around, though mostly, as I recall, from 'outsiders'. For instance, there was the case of Effie Wadd, the Revd Hayward's young maid, just up from Wales. This happened about the summer of 1913, as I recall that I was still walking from Townsend to Randwick school daily, and, during the absence of the vicar and Mrs Hayward, I was sent by my father to keep Effie company for the night. After climbing the long stairs to the attic, lit only by the light from a flickering wax candle, we eventually got to bed and went to sleep, only to be awakened around midnight by a fierce thunderstorm. Effie was terrified by this *force majeure*, and rushed around covering up mirrors to prevent a lightning strike, or thunderball as it was then called. When a sharp 'crack' sounded on the front window, Effie insisted that our time had come! She made me trudge downstairs, where we prostrated ourselves in the hallway, and prayed for forgiveness of past sins.

Much to our surprise, our prayer was immediately answered by a loud knocking at the front door, and who should enter but my own dear father. Apparently he had been throwing gravel up at the window to attract our attention in case we were frightened. He reassured us, provided warm clothes and, as we trudged all the way down to

MISS TARA PROVIDES CURTSY LESSONS
—BUT THE SCHOOL CAT IS NOT IMPRESSED.

Townsend, Effie was heard to repeat 'We have been forgiven our sins, and the Lord has saved us'.

The village school was then run by Mr Mortimer as head, assisted by the Misses Fox and Cain, known unofficially as 'Cane and Mabel'. Actually Mr Mortimer, a serious but kindly man, did all the caning – only once, I am glad to report, in my case. Generally subjects consisted of the four R's, 'reading, 'riting, 'rithmetic, and religion', but a fair amount of geography and history was taught, notably regarding the Feudal System. One Friday afternoon we actually had readings from *Jason and the Argonauts*, which was quite striking in the midst of the Cotswolds, and I have never ceased to admire Jason, the somewhat

MRS PEACOCK DISTRIBUTES LARGESSE,
- CLOSELY ASSISTED BY 'MISS EMILY'.

casual leader, as opposed to the more purposeful Ulysses. Practical subjects included dressmaking, in which I excelled.

Compared with the large-scale sophistication of the modern comprehensive school, I suppose we were relatively easily satisfied in those days, and I can recall nothing more pleasant than Saints' Days when we attended church and then had the day free, though the climax of the school year was Empire Day when we sang patriotic songs for the school governors, all decked out with red, white and blue rosettes, prior to being presented with a bun, an orange and a penny, and dismissed for the day.

School summer holidays were relatively short in those days and we

18

were usually kept well occupied with errands or church duties. Saturday afternoons were for shopping and when my father returned from work after the long walk from Stroud, he would dine and then walk with Arthur and I all the way back to Stonehouse for household supplies. Fortunately the roads were empty of traffic and we could safely walk down the centre of Stonehouse High Street.

Sundays were for churchgoing but, as my father and brothers were in the choir, and we lived immediately opposite, this did not seem at all unnatural. There were also some surprisingly cultured people in the congregation, including the erudite Amanda Powell who played organ and sang solos on festive occasions. She lived with her parents and sisters Cissy, Laura, and Constance, in an old weaver's cottage adjoining the site of the present War Memorial, and was an authority on natural history as well as the classical authors.

Sunday school started at ten o'clock and even included lessons in the social graces! We were encouraged to say 'Good Morning, Miss Tara' to our teacher, and curtsy, if girls. This was doubtless intended to stand us in good stead in our later vocations. At Morning Service we would sit with Miss Tara in our best pinnies and bonnets, behind the choir stalls, and look very superior. After Matins my father, suitably dressed in dark suit and bowler, would take me to visit his parents, who then lived at Cashes Green, whilst mother prepared lunch. He dutifully took a meat pie or pudding and I was duly seated upon my special stool, whilst Gran Fletcher presented me with a tin of iced biscuits, from which I was allowed to select two. She was a serious personality, but Grandad was great fun. I suppose bringing up ten children over a period of thirty-five years had left her somewhat 'drained'.

After lunch, my father would take Arthur and I for a walk in the woods, accompanied by our puppy, Nero, during which he would extol the beauties of nature. Then it was High Tea and Evensong.

Nero was a small black-and-tan Manchester terrier which Uncle Jess procured for us. He was aptly named and regarded himself as the 'light of the universe'. One Sunday evening when we had all gone to church, he escaped by jumping from a first floor window, entered the church during the sermon and sat quietly next to our pew at the back. He was duly ejected when he tried to join in the final hymn.

A daunting aspect of Sunday school was the compulsory learning of a collect, which took Arthur and myself most of Saturday evening to assimilate, but at Christmas book prizes were given for good behaviour and attendance. This was a social event held at the day school, and started with a tea consisting of bread and butter, slab cake and lemonade, followed by the prizegiving, and concluding with a concert party.

LED BY THE DRUM AND FIFE BAND, RANDWICK SUNDAY SCHOOL WHITSUN PARADE
CIRCLES LONGCOURT LAKE — MY BROTHERS FRED & ARTHUR ATTEND REV. HAYWARD

The church choir had a separate outing during the summer and, as relatives were invited, I experienced my first trip to the seaside at Weston-super-Mare, by courtesy of the Great Western Railway.

The main event in the social calendar, however, was the Sunday school Whitsun Parade. This commenced when we formed up in the school playground after lunch, girls in best white pinafores and bonnets, boys in Norfolk suits with caps. In good military order, by classes, and led by the drum-and-fife band, we marched down to Longcourt House, then circled the lake and climbed the long drive up to the Rylands, where we were received by Colonel and Mrs Anderson before proceeding to the fête field above the vicarage. There Fred Turner the burly churchwarden, my father and others would have erected the usual sideshows, which were stored in the vicarage attics, and we ran races, with one penny prizes, and competed in scrambles for sweets. The day usually finished with a cricket match, in which the men played the boys. A very auspicious occasion. Later, carnivals were held in Chapel Fields on Midsummer's Day, but I had left home by this time.

Father, Arthur and I walking down Stonehouse High Street c. 1909.

21

LIFE AROUND HOME

My father, though strict, was energetically provident, and my mother was all that a mother could be. My elder brother, Fred, was a serious philosophical boy, who doubtless would have made a mark in some field of creativity, had he survived the Great War.

My younger brother Arthur, being but two years my junior and full of practical mischief, was great company and eventually made a successful career as an executive engineer. Sister Phyllis was a quiet, sensitive girl and being seven years my junior, I suppose I was more her nursemaid than playmate at this stage.

One Saturday, to my relief, I was sent by mother to Cainscross to buy provisions, in charge of a whole gold sovereign. After making several purchases at the Co-op, I called on Mr Beard the butcher to buy a pig's head, which my mother required to make brawn. (Actually my father kept a 'pig in the yard' at Townsend, but this he usually sold to Mr Beard.) Shopping completed, I pocketed a half-sovereign change, and made for home.

Whilst passing through the Townsend playing field, I was approached by schoolfriends saying 'gin us a look'. Inquisitively they inspected the half-sovereign and counted the pig's teeth and, during the meleé, the coin disappeared into the long grass. It was never found, and I have always regretted the loss, but my mother never punished me and my father worked harder than ever at his part-time occupations, to remedy the loss of half a week's wages.

As I approached school-leaving age I was often required to perform modest tasks at the vicarage. On one occasion, when Effie was on home leave, I was asked to 'caretake' for a few hours, and receive callers. Crime was practically unknown locally and, when a respectably dressed young man called and desired to view the church interior I trustingly loaned him the key. Unfortunately, he never returned, and next day the offertory box was found ransacked. I was duly quizzed by the constable

Our cottage at Townsend.

and, to my relief, a few days later a man was caught in a similar act at a church nearby. When the case was heard by Gloucester magistrates, I had to appear to identify the culprit, which I did, with some trepidation.

Before the advent of regular public services, communal spirit was rarely lacking when needed. One night, after we had all retired, we were awakened by a loud crackling noise and looked out to see the wood on fire. As the westerly wind made this dangerous to nearby cottages, my father tolled the church bell to raise the alarm. Almost immediately, the entire village turned out, complete with buckets. Two human chains

Grandfather Emmanuel's cottage.

Mr Baxter's bakery at Townsend.

24

A vandal-proof stone stile at Townsend.

were formed and attached to the village pond nearby, one passing full buckets, whilst the other returned the empties. This operation went on well into the night, until all was safe.

This was not an isolated example. There was, for instance, the case of 'Nero's Rescue'.

This dog was, after all, a bit of a nuisance and, but for our child-like concern, might not have been seriously missed! However, after some four days inexplicable absence, the men turned out to make a thorough search of the Ash, where he had last been seen. Eventually he was heard whining deep down a rabbit warren and duly dug out, much to our relief. Unfortunately, during his incarceration he developed a taste for Cotswold limestone which never completely left him, and of which he eventually died. Poor old Nero. He was such a pet, even when he ate the cherries from my new straw hat.

Later, as a result of my father's craftsmanship, I received an elegant doll's carriage and brother Fred a super trolley. The latter linked up

THE 'RANDWICK FLYER' HURTLES PAST LONGCOURT
— HOTLY PURSUED BY NERO AND 'THE LAW'.

rather conveniently with my mother's duties as Postmistress as, having a phone, and telegraphs being expensive, we were in great demand to deliver telephone messages to friends and neighbours. As they mostly lived downhill at Townsend or Cashes Green, this provided an ideal opportunity to 'show our paces' with the trolley and was not particularly dangerous, on account of the almost total absence of vehicular traffic. With Fred as driver, Arthur as brake man, and myself as 'ballast', we could make the one mile run to Cashes Green in five minutes dead! The pull back up was not so exhilarating but, as we usually received a small reward, we would spend this at Mrs Cole's sweet shop on our return home. On one occasion, when I was not present, brother Fred unfortunately knocked the constable off his bike and was severely chastised by my father. During the winter we often made the same trip by sledge.

My mother's best friend, Mrs Crocker, was dourly statuesque. We kids were quite scared of her, though she was very good-hearted. She

26

MRS. CROCKER ARRIVES WITH AN INTERESTING
PACKAGE — & NERO DISGRACES HIMSELF.

was a typical private service housekeeper of the old school – reliable,
self-sufficient, and somewhat imperious. Doubtless her more diplo-
matic employers went in awe of her. She was now a widow and retired,
and dressed completely in black as if she had never left mourning. Her
chief claim to fame, and the apple of her eye, was a brother in Australia,
a sheep-farmer who sent her a whole lamb occasionally. This was a
major event locally as, having sold the choice parts to Mr Beard to
augment her income, she would generously distribute the lesser cuts to
her friends and neighbours, including my mother. We kids could
therefore predict when we might be served lamb on weekdays (joints
being normally reserved for Sundays only) if we noted the carrier's

27

visits. Dear old Mrs Crocker. She went to live at Dudbridge eventually, and we lost touch.

Mr Monsell was the local *éminence grise* – a true lateral thinker who lived with his wife, a local doctor's daughter, in the cottage next door to the Post Office. He held commissioned rank in the army during the war, but afterwards worked locally in mill management. His *metier* was an encyclopaedic knowledge and gift for practical mechanics, coupled with a benign interest in children, partly, I suspect, because he had none of his own. With a couple of cocoa tins and some wire he would demonstrate the principle of the telephone for our entertainment.

MANNERS

AND

ATTITUDES

U nlike Gwen Raverat's delightful tales of Cambridge 'moral atti-
tudes', I cannot report that Randwick was at all sophisticated in
comparison. Indeed, the general level of moral behaviour prescribed by
the Church was well observed both publicly and privately.

As employment was partly rural and partly industrial, politics were
moderate, and the fairly equal division which obtained around the time
of the Civil Wars, when the country areas were generally Royalist and
the larger boroughs Parliamentarian, was still broadly applicable.
Emotions ran high at election time and skill at the hustings was still
essential to a politician. With a large Chapel population in the vicinity,
MPs have always had to work for votes. It was following the
unsuccessful siege of Parliamentarian Gloucester in 1643 that Charles I
was to advise his sons to 'prepare for the worst'.

Girls married young and, despite the total lack of formal sex
education in those days, managed to produce some remarkably healthy
children. There were, admittedly, a few 'shotgun' marriages, but the
(modern) term 'single parent family' really only applied to widows and
widowers, and even these usually remarried. Flora Bennett, for
instance, was past her second marriage when I knew her, having two
children by her first husband and three by her second. My mother
never cared to remarry, but she had the Post Office and a small pension
for support, and later chose to live with each of her children in turn.

Occasional extra-marital romance occurred, as I was to find out later
when I became aware of such matters. Whilst I am not suggesting that I
was typical, I have no regrets regarding my style of upbringing, with the
exception that we girls might have been warned about the
circumstances surrounding puberty. If the average village child knew
too little about sex, I imagine some of the middle class girls knew even
less. I recall the case of a respected local young lady who married a
military man on the conclusion of the Great War and, in due course,

gave birth to tiny stillborn twins. I was amazed when Flora told me, in strict confidence, that the lady in question didn't even know she was pregnant, or how she became so! On the other hand there were, occasionally, mysterious 'goings on' when lanterns were placed in windows at night to signal local girls that the coast was clear for an assignation. But this was most unusual.

With the exception of occasional 'outsider baddies', theft and graft never occurred and life was too hard to risk one's money on betting. Except for the occasional drunkard, wives and families were invariably well treated.

As there was nothing in the way of street lighting in those days, nice girls just didn't go out after dark, except on summer evenings when the boys played 'will-o-the-wisp' with lanterns in the gloaming. Mothers still disciplined their children with the caution that 'old Boney will get you if you're bad', and this seemed to work, despite the fact that 'old Boney' had been dead for some seventy years by this time. I suppose our grandparents were cautioned in this manner and, in the isolation of the country, the threat was passed on.

Randwick folk were fairly laconic and I can't recall any great conversationalists, or indeed scandal-mongers, though I can't say what happened in the pubs.

I don't recall a strong Gloucestershire accent, though the boys sometimes adopted strange declensions of the verb 'to be'. This ran as follows:

> I *be*
> Thee *bist*
> He, She, It *bist*
> We *be*
> You *be*
> They *be*
> (The negative was generally *bissent*.)

Boys also used such phrases as 'were be gwine?', or 'were bist thee gwine?', but we girls knew better.

Modest bullying went on at school, though mostly of the minor 'catty' type between girls, and was quickly forgotten. Men were invariably polite to women and both were considerate to children.

Concerning strange word-usage, my own mother referred to the C of E hymn book as 'Ancient and Moderate', and Hardy's famous novel as 'Far from the Maddening Crowd', but whether 'tongue-in-cheek' I never discovered.

Despite laconic tendencies, however, the propensity for practical joking was considerable, especially among the younger men. Flora Bennett, being a public figure and very good-natured, was especially susceptible. Sometimes she was sent to attend local VIPs who weren't in need of her services, and occasionally, on light-hearted matters, she was caused to fail to attend when needed. On one occasion, when Revd Hayward paid a courtesy call he knocked upon the door of her tiny cottage for some minutes whilst Flora repeated drowsily from her armchair 'Don't 'ee think oi be a'comin' to answer 'ee this time moi lad', believing the caller to be her jovial sailor son Fred, 'having her on' yet again. The imperturbable vicar, with typical diplomacy, departed in silence, much to Flora's dismay when she eventually found out the truth of the matter.

On another occasion, when a local lady had a fainting fit after climbing up to the Ash, Flora immediately rushed to render first aid by means of a large bottle of brandy, much to the concern of the local GP who considered smelling salts much more appropriate. She had a great fund of stories of local events and would often hold forth with her eyes half closed and arms folded, leaning back against her kitchen table. I only wish I could remember them now.

SOCIAL LIFE

Dress

O nce again, I cannot possibly compete with Gwen Raverat with an inventory of eight foundation undergarments! Starting from inside, women wore a cotton chemise, long bloomers to the knee, high stiff corsets and black woollen stockings. Over this were several long underskirts, according to weather conditions, shaped blouse, and long heavy top skirt. Large black straw hats and short button boots were usual. Overcoats were long, dark and shaped. Makeup was unheard of. Boys wore Norfolk jackets and knee breeches, with long woollen stockings and boots, over shirt and underclothes, and men wore Norfolk jackets and 'drainpipe' trousers. Braces were essential to the 'cut', and belts were occasionally worn *as well*. Flat caps, bowlers, or straw boaters in summer were essential – how else could one salute a lady! Workmen wore good tweeds, exchanging their jackets for overalls at work, and always kept one suit for Sunday best – so much more dignified than the universal jeans of today. The gentry dressed very similarly, with the addition of sticks and gloves for the men, and more foundation garments and exceptionally large hats, heavily decorated, for the ladies. Indeed, the size of these confections tended to increase with rank, with the squire's lady and the vicar's wife in keen competition!

I cannot remember a really badly dressed person – threadbare perhaps – but the county still manufactured the best worsted suiting in the world. Later, local firms were bought up by north-country combines and put on to manufacturing green baise and tennis-ball cloth.

Women's fashions before suffrage were extremely dignified, demanding large bosoms and hips with wasp waists, whereas after suffrage, and the Great War, fashion dictated small busts, narrow hips and long legs. It was almost as if women were glad to adopt a more feminine style – but only after obtaining the vote.

Behaviour

Generally *decorum* was the thing to be aimed at, both for children and adults. The British 'stiff upper lip' was still generally admired. Even children didn't cry – at least not in public – and they *never* spoke at meals! This was somewhat restricting but, as we had so much to say away from the dining table and adult conversation was generally boring, it didn't matter too much. 'Grace' at meals was practically mandatory, but not family prayers.

Religion and the Arts

Practically all went to church at least once on Sunday and singing styles varied from my friend Amanda Powell's near professional soprano, developed in the Stroud Choral Society, to the more nasal contralto of the female majority. Men sang a good base-baritone. Some played musical instruments in the home, mostly for 'song accompaniment'. My brother Arthur, for instance, sang and played accordian and, suitably dressed in a Pierrot outfit which I made, often won prizes at the summer carnivals in Chapel Fields. Sister Phyllis and I both took piano lessons at Stroud once a week, though she had an embarrassing habit of sitting down on the pavement outside and refusing to budge until so directed by Miss Cresswell. Poor girl, she really was more talented than her shyness permitted at that time.

Sociability

School friends were numerous, but uppermost in my mind are Winnie Aston, Emily Watkins, Gertie Broomfield, Jo Brain, Hilda Sprout, Georgina Bassett and Lucy Lugg. After school Winnie, Emily and I would walk to Sandpits, where they lived in a cluster of cottages nestling in the shelter of the Ash, and where I was invariably invited to tea with Winnie and her aunt. It is reassuring to recall how pleasant such a modest cottage could be with its sheltering atmosphere and colourful walled garden.

Gerty and Jo lived at Westrip in adjoining cottages and here I was also sure of a welcome. Poor Jo lost her father in the war, the first to be lost to the village, leaving just she and her mother to mourn. I'm glad to recount that, in later years, Jo was to marry Dick Barnett of Whiteshill, and so become my sister's 'in-law'.

33

Weavers cottages and Amanda Powell's house (left).

Hilda Sprout lived at Townsend with her grandmother, Mrs Giles. When she and I were about eleven years old, arrangements were made to have our adenoids removed, in accord with current medical practice. We walked to Stroud hospital in the early morning and were duly anaesthetised with ether on gauze masks. Later that day I awoke to sounds of whimpering and found myself amongst many other children, lying on the bare floor and feeling pretty sick. Hilda and I were most relieved when Mr Harmer, complete with 'hearse', came to take us home! I quickly recovered, but Hilda suffered a haemorrhage and had to be returned to hospital for aftercare.

Randwick School

NEWLY CONFIRMED WE PASS THE TOWN HALL WITH HIGH HOPES

35

Randwick School caretaker's cottage – now the Post Office.

Georgina Bassett lived in the upper part of Randwick, near to the Vine Tree Inn. She was a quiet girl of kindly disposition and had also lost her father. We were confirmed together by the Bishop of Gloucester at Stroud Parish Church in 1917, in home-made white muslin dresses and veils. The church was packed, and it was a memorable occasion. After the Armistice, Georgina and her mother both emigrated to America and, after sixty-six years, we still correspond.

Lucy Lugg lived with her parents, five brothers and four sisters in a cottage next to the weavers' houses. They were a happy family and three of the boys, William, Henry and Walter, were to serve in the Great

36

HILDA WAITS FOR ANISEED BALLS WHILST NERO
TAKES A SURREPTITIOUS LICK FROM MY TOFFEE APPLE
IN MRS. COLES' SWEETSHOP AT LAUREL COTTAGE.

War, William being awarded the DCM. Lucy still lives in the vicinity with her many grandchildren.

I suppose our favourite activity after school, if we had a penny, was to visit Mrs Cole's sweet shop at Laurel Cottage. She was a small woman, dressed in a black full-length skirt and blouse, with a spotless starched white apron, and showed a kindly patience whilst we hesitated over the 'best buy'. For one penny, one could obtain no less than four items in

37

ADA SKINNER IN 'FULL REGALIA'

those days; for instance, a strip of liquorice, a gob-stopper, aniseed balls, and a packet of sherbert! This delightful trade is now transferred to the new Post Office opposite and Laurel Cottage is occupied by Margaret Parish, daughter of my late friends Dan and Dorothy Nott, and who provides 'cottage accommodation'.

Whilst at Mrs Cole's we would visit Ada Skinner who lived at the school caretaker's house opposite. She was in her teens and did much of the school cleaning for her mother, but on account of her large size and good nature, came in for a certain amount of chaffing from we children. She never once reproved us but merely gave as good as she received in verbal repartee.

Before the Second World War, milk wasn't generally delivered, so it fell to the children to collect it daily in a special small can which was usually stored in the kitchen, against the cool back wall. With Vicks at Westrip, Jordans at Humphries End, and the Phipps at Longcourt Farm, the young emissary had a choice of patronage. On a fine day, one might even struggle up to Bassett's farm above the Rising Sun, where apples were presented as a bonus in season. Whilst there, one might look in on Mr Townley, the village cobbler, in his tiny cluttered workshop behind the pub. The milk was delicious, and we never experienced any problems with lack of sterilization.

Later friends were Maud and Doris Blanch and Emily Pearce. In after years Maud married Giles Bassett and lived in a cottage at Cox Gate, below the Methodist chapel. She was talented, energetic and pleasantly attractive and served as organist at the chapel right up to her death in her mid-eighties. Emily Pearce never married but lived alone at Townsend and regularly attended Randwick church until her death. Doris Blanch later married Ted Barnett, the brother of Fred who was to marry my sister Phyllis.

School dinners weren't available before the Second World War, but I was lucky in that living near school I was able to walk home comfortably at mid-day. Monday was always wash-day, a day of domestic activity not particularly favoured by we children, as lunch generally consisted of Sunday leftovers. We breakfasted early and I 'serviced' and folded away into trunks my father's and brothers' Sunday suits, whilst mother stoked up the copper in the outbuilding for the day's wash.

The 'routine week' for we kids was from Tuesday to Friday, as Saturday was 'bath day' and involved stoking up the copper once again. Baths were taken in turn in a hip bath near the copper, following which my brother Arthur and I would sit in front of the kitchen fire and rehearse our collect for Sunday school, whilst my mother curled my damp hair with strips of white calico, to conjure a mass of auburn curls for the Sabbath. At that time drinking water was carried from Pool Spring nearby and washing water from our two rainwater butts.

The gentry survived largely socially intact at least until the Second World War though, unlike Gwen Raverat, we would not have described a lady as 'one who didn't do anything for herself'. In fact most local ladies cooked or gardened a little, whilst their husbands farmed or hunted. I suppose the dividing line was that of property ownership rather than income level, though even here, estates and houses were often rented and, in times of difficulty, mortgaged. Nevertheless the divide between 'landed' and 'tradesman' was generally appreciated and, being so, ceased to be an issue and engendered a degree of mutual respect.

Schoolfriends and workmates were 'for keeps', and it was only the necessity of earning a living outside the village that finally separated us. It must have been *really* self-contained and 'cosy' before the advent of steam-power caused the demise of the independant home weaver – like those who lived in the Church Lane cottages during the last century.

SATURDAY BATHNIGHT - WITH CURLERS & COLLECTS
(THIS PROVES THAT CLEANLINESS IS NEXT TO GODLINESS)
- ARTHUR TRIES ON HIS NEW CHOIR 'SHIMMY'.

Romance

Needless to say, courtships developed locally, often with partners from
the nearby villages. I recall with admiration that life-long partnership
between my old friends Harold Robinson and Amy Hogg of Randwick

who met, I believe, at a football match in Stroud, where Harold played for Uplands and Amy was a Randwick supporter.

For the more reticent, reading romantic novels by candelight was a favourite winter's occupation and the local Stroud library kept a good stock of Dickens, Trollope, and the Brontës, as well as more popular novels. Unfortunately the editions available to us were usually in small typeface and probably didn't do our eyesight much good.

UNCLES AND AUNTS — AND COUSIN WILL

B y the time I was about halfway through school, I became aware that
my mother's father had died and that Gran Birt had retired to the
Pershore area, where my mother's sister Jane and her husband Bill
Clarke had a small fruit farm. The latter had always intrigued me as,
every year in season, we received a hamper of fine apples and plums
from this source, and I vividly imagined an Arcadia of lush orchards in
the sheltered Severn valley, very different from our steep and stony hill
country.

In the autumn of 1913 I was delighted to hear that my mother, sister
and I were to visit our Birt relatives for the week-end. My father was to
stay at home to look after the Post Office, as there were still Saturday
and Sunday deliveries and collections at this period. This was sad in the
event as due to the war and its aftermath, my father was never to make
this trip. However, blissfully unaware of this, we set out early on
Saturday morning to walk to Dudbridge station, some two miles away,
and caught the Midland Railways 'Dudbridge Donkey' to Gloucester.
We duly changed lines to the Great Western for Worcester, then
changed for Fladbury, to complete all of twenty-five miles as the crow
flies. After another two-mile walk we arrived exhausted at Gran Birt's
cottage, situated in a narrow alley in Pershore town.

Compared with Gran Pollard, she was a tiny woman, still dressed
completely in mourning black, with bonnet tied under her chin and
sitting in a rocking chair. She was totally blind, but very glad to receive
us. She was probably born soon after Queen Victoria's accession and
here, at least, time was transfixed – but not for long, as that evening we
walked to Uncle Bill's farm at Lower Moor. They were a large family
with a large house to match! My cousins consisted of two girls and four
boys, including cousin Will – and you could count him as two at least!

On Sunday afternoon, when I was feeling somewhat in need of
solitude, my sister and I ventured to try the swing which my uncle had

42

GRAN BINT IN HER TINY 'ALLEY' COTTAGE AT PERSHORE — TOTALLY BLIND — WITH HER SOLE REGULAR COMPANION

rigged up in the orchard. As I climbed higher and higher in the sweet summer air, I imagined I was bearing the Golden Fleece across the Hellespont when, unbeknown to me, I was actually flying free – only to awake with a jolt as I landed in a large lavender bush. Cousin Will, hiding in the tree, had cut the swing rope! I arrived home that evening, tired and bruised, carrying a large basket of Victoria plums.

Soon after this visit I heard, with some trepidation, that Cousin Will was to stay with us for some months as a 'disciplinary' measure! Some hope, I thought, though in the event we probably had some small influence upon him.

One winter's night, soon after his arrival, when we had been discussing ghosts at supper, Phyllis and I were fast asleep when I became aware of an ominous scratching sound under the bed. I lay very still and froze but, upon repetition of this psychic phenomena, I must have screamed, for my dear mother arrived with a candle to drag out the

'SPOT' WATCHES EXPECTANTLY AS COUSIN WILL
CUTS THE SWING ROPE AT AUNT JANE'S

offending 'spirit', in the form of Cousin Will. This was the only
occasion I recall when my father resorted to corporal punishment.

Of my father's brothers, Uncle Tom was my favourite. He was a big
amiable man, the last of the Victorian 'polymaths', and a little eccentric.
As his wife was generally chairbound with rheumatism, and advised
against childbirth, they took a kindly interest in their nephews and

44

—AND TO MY INTENSE RELIEF MY DEAR MOTHER INVESTIGATES THE 'POST OFFICE GHOST'.

UNCLE TOM & ME ON THE 'CONVEYANCE' CLOSELY FOLLOWED BY 'CROMWELL'

ATTENDED BY EFFIE WADD, VICAR BOARDS UNCLE
JESS'S CROSSLEY - & NERO CONTEMPLATES A CHASE

neices and I was often invited to spend the school holidays with them at Trowbridge. This trip was a classic event, as I was allowed to ride all the way from Randwick in Aunt Lucy's 'conveyance'. This was a standard bicycle with 'outrigger' and a basket chair attached, and was quite a pleasant way of touring in fine weather.

At Trowbridge Uncle ran a nursery garden, plus an orchard with a flock of milking goats and billy, as well as an insurance agency 'on the side'. The travel required for the latter, plus my aunt's interest in herbal medicine, caused him to develop an encyclopaedic knowledge of plants and he combined this with extensive reading in the arts and sciences.

Their spaniel dog Nell was an old friend and accompanied them on cycle rides, and Poll the parrot was a great mimic. He was so quick to learn that on one occasion the baker, hearing (as he thought) my aunt say 'No bread today baker', in fact declined to leave any, much to our surprise! He would also join in hymn-singing on Sunday evening, which my uncle accompanied on violin. I thoroughly enjoyed my holidays at Trowbridge, as well as gaining general knowledge.

Later, when motorcycles became available, my uncle bought a Red Indian complete with brass fuel tank and Indian head symbol, but this lacked the charm (and reliability) of the 'conveyance'.

46

My second favourite uncle was Uncle Jess. After long years of service with the British army in India and the Middle East as a Serjeant Major, he had become somewhat more august than either my father or Uncle Tom and as he did not retire from the regular army till around 1912, I did not meet him previously. He married Aunt Jane, who was in the Nursing Service, in India and they were totally devoted to each other, but had no children. When he retired the Service, they set up a general stores in Dursley, and later a second-hand furniture store. As I was later to live with them as assistant, I will describe this in due course.

When I first met him he was in full Regimentals, complete with spurs, as he had taken a temporary post as a recruiting sergeant at Gloucester at the outbreak of war. His pride and joy at this time was a second-hand car which he had purchased from the Bishop of Gloucester and used as a taxi and for weddings. His main aim seemed to be to get volunteers for the army amongst family and friends! My father, as a vehicle smith, was an early recruit to the 'MT' section of the Army Service Corps, and my brother Fred was later to enter the Royal West Kents as a signalman.

Aunt Florence Wilkins was something of an enigma. She was the miller's daughter at Bourton, where she met and became espoused to my Uncle Eli who was killed in the Boer War. They had a son, Albert, who later married Georgina Wenman of Bampton, and this was how I met, and married, her brother Bill. Cousin Albert died young, but Georgina lived until 1976, raising a family of five on her own resources, all of whom prospered. They lived in the old caretaker's cottage at Stonehouse Brushworks and my visits were chiefly memorable for the sight of young Bill Wenman in his naval uniform, but they were also the occasion of much mirth. Cousin Albert was then a slight youth and, as was generally predicted, might one day get 'lost down the loo'. This was no idle threat as the 'loo' in question was for the convenience of the workmen and was cantilevered conveniently over the Mill stream on a rickety gantry. Unlike Sir John Mills' childhood experience, if one fell through the 'large hole' of *this* one, the result was probably death by drowning! I frankly went in fear of using it and was glad to get home to our own cesspool WC. This didn't have a cistern, but a bucket flush was kept handy. Doubtless a modern sanitary inspector would condemn it out of hand.

SHADOWS

OF

WAR

By 1914 my brother Fred had started work at the office of the *Stroud Journal* as a junior reporter. I was twelve, and beginning to evade duties as nursemaid to my younger sister. This was doubly welcome as Arthur and I could, at weekends, explore that gaslit brick and stone rabbit-warren called Stroud, as it entered the modern era practically direct from the Middle Ages! To be fair, it did receive George III (on horse) in 1788, and Isambard Kingdom Brunel (by rail) in 1845 but, other than the myriad small woollen-mills which studded the Frome Valley (and which were practically a cottage industry), the ambivalent benefits of non-automated mass production were only just arriving.

We children were intrigued by the development of electric light, telephone and wireless telegraphy, but particularly by the heady disclosures at 'Spots' Cinema in Lansdown – if we could obtain the required 3*d* entrance fee.

Stroud was particularly fortunate in having sufficient local families of imagination and financial standing, including the Playnes, Grists, and Holloways, to wrench it quickly into the twentieth century. George Holloway, a great entrepreneur, founded the 'Steam Sewing Works' in Threadneedle Street in 1854, chiefly to make corduroy trousers for the railway navvies. This was where I was to obtain my first job on leaving school in 1916. He died in 1892 and was Chairman of the Mid-Gloucester Conservative Working Men's Benefit Society, with the motto 'God helps those who help themselves' – such was the relatively uncomplicated nature of management/worker relations at that time.

George Holloway doubtless received inspiration from the shining example of Edwin Budding who, not to be outdone by Robert Stephenson's design for the Rocket in 1829, invented the cylinder lawn-mower the following year, by enlarging the cloth shears which he used in his mill design shop to herculean proportions. He recommended it 'for the exercise of gentlemen on their country estates' and

IMPROVED MOWING MACHINES,

MANUFACTURED BY

JAMES FERRABEE & Co.,

PHŒNIX IRON WORKS,

NEAR STROUD,

GLOUCESTERSHIRE.

THESE MOWING MACHINES can be used by unskilled labourers with equal facility on Lawns, Verges, between Flower Beds, on Bowling Greens, Cricket and Pleasure Grounds. The Machines are fitted with every attention to strength and durability, and are not liable to get out of order. The 28 inch and 36 inch Machines are made very strong, and will cut the longest and coarsest grass usually met with on Lawns and Pleasure Grounds. They execute their work in an expeditious and superior manner, producing a more even and uniform surface than the most skilful mower, and are readily adjusted to cut various lengths. The grass is cut best when dry, so that a machine can be employed at the most convenient time to the workman, and more than double the work may be done with the same manual labour that is requisite with a scythe. Upwards of 5000 of them have been manufactured at the above works.

Price List,—

Including Carriage to any Railway Station South of York.

			£	s.	d.
Hand Machine, for One Man,	cutting 16 inches wide....		5	10	0
Ditto, for Man and Boy,	„ 22 ditto..........		6	0	0
Pony Machine (or Donkey),	„ 26 ditto..........		8	0	0
Horse Machine,	„ 28 ditto		11	0	0
Ditto,	„ 36 ditto		15	0	0

SOLD BY

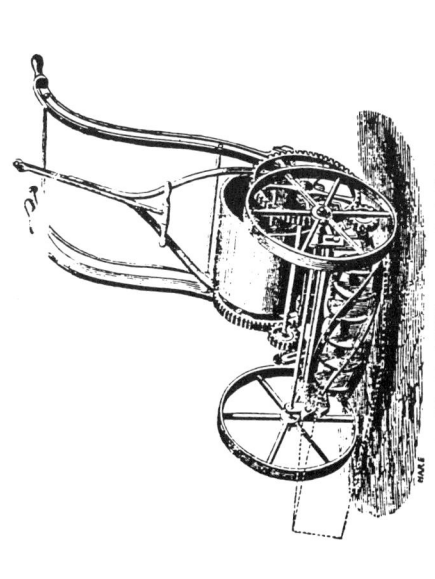

HAND MACHINE.—*One Inch Scale.*

HORSE MACHINE.—*Half-Inch Scale.*

The commercial development of Budding's patent. (Illustration by courtesy of Lionel Walrond, Curator of Stroud Museum)

STROUD CENTRE FROM PARK GARDENS TODAY – LITTLE CHANGED IN 80 YEARS

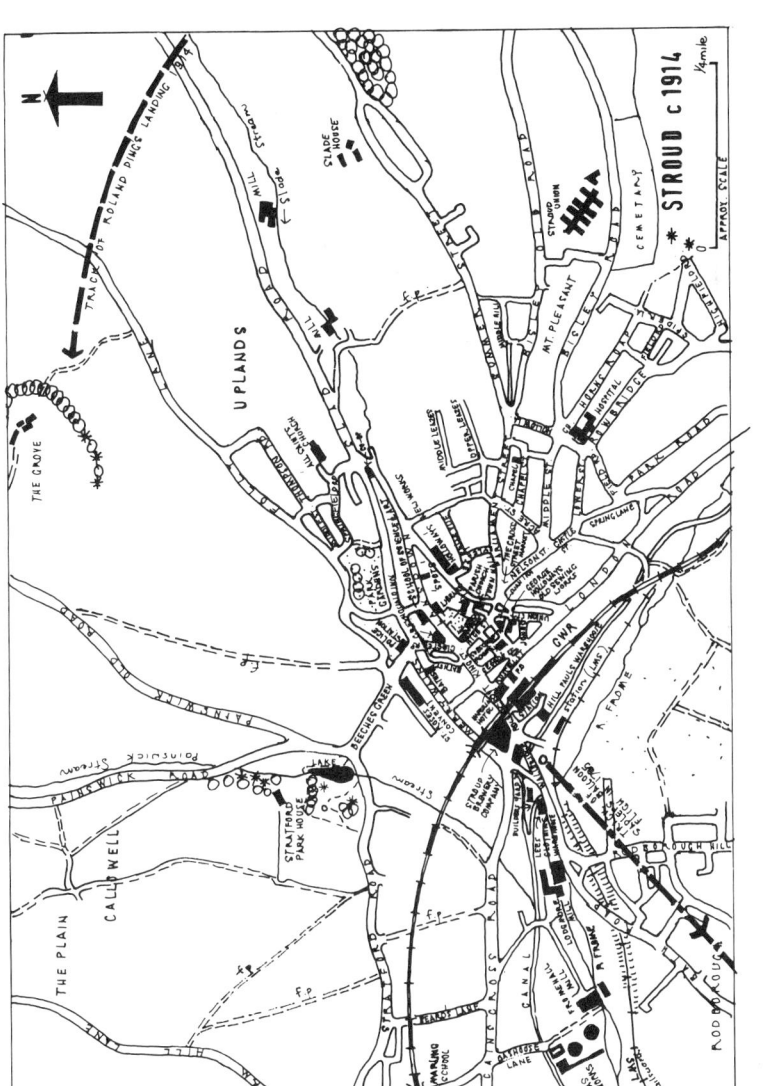

STROUD c 1914

¼ mile
APPROX SCALE

N

TRACK OF ROLAND PING'S LANDING 1914

THE GROVE

THE PLAIN

CALLOWELL

UPLANDS

SLADE HOUSE

MILL STREAM

STRATFORD PARK HOUSE

PAINSWICK STREAM

MT PLEASANT

STROUD UNION

CEMETERY

CWA

'The pioneer aviator W. Rowland Ding, who took his pilot training with the Beatty School of Flying at Hendon, and attained his "brevet" from the Royal Aero Club on the 28th April 1914, after only 3 hours instruction.' (by courtesy of Flight Magazine, 22 May 1914)

W. Roland Ding's Handley Page Scimitar at Hendon in 1914.

could not have forseen the modern 'postage-stamp' suburban lawn. Stroud has usually shown keen interest in scientific development and, in 1795, Sadler made his pioneer balloon ascent from Wallbridge, only two years after the first Paris flight.

During the war my mother took two weekly magazines, each costing one penny, called *The Tailoress and Dress Cutter*, and *Our Home*. Besides short stories, children's serial, social chat page, and 'agony' column, these provided dressmaking instructions and a paper pattern from which, with the aid of my mother's old Singer, I was quickly to adopt the craft of dressmaking, to be developed later by lessons at the Stroud School of Art and Science. This was a remarkable 'Florentine Gothic' building in Lansdown, built in 1899 in an attempt to marry the best of the useful arts and sciences before they fragmented, and which covered various subjects from photography to book-keeping. It is significant that it has a row of portrait heads at first floor level which depict Faraday, Huxley, Kelvin, Barry, Rosetti, Leighton and Turner, as I recall – three scientists and three artists surrounding an architect – perhaps the last monument to urban sanity.

But my pride and joy, purchased for me by my father during his first home leave from the army, was a new Raleigh bike, complete with three speed gears and dress guard, and upon which I was to make many pioneering trips accompanied by my brother Arthur.

Our innocent lifestyle had been little changed by the outbreak of war in August 1914 but with the rush of young men to volunteer, and our increasing involvement in what were considered to be male occupations, we had little time to sorrow. The issues involved did not particularly concern us, as we had little knowledge of, or interest in, the politics of Eastern Europe. Military service was organised on a local or even family basis and even the top politicians and generals could not envisage the effect of modern technology to create static, terrible, and useless trench warfare. In any case the whole thing was to be over by Christmas. . . .

A lively diversion shortly before war was declared was the aircraft landing at Uplands by W. Rowland Ding on the 16th June 1914. He flew a Handley-Page Scimitar bi-plane, with a 100 h.p. Anzani engine, and completed his first major flight from London to Bath on the 26th May 1914. He landed at Uplands, apparently due to lack of fuel, on the 16th June, departing on the 18th. He and his passenger trudged into Stroud with gallon cans for petrol, and Mr W.H. Knight and my brother-in-law, Fred Barnett, were eyewitnesses. Unfortunately, owing to spy-fever then current, this epic was generally regarded as 'enemy-inspired' amongst the more impressionable.

PART II
WAR
AND
AFTERMATH

Fred Pollard in uniform.

LEAVING
SCHOOL

A s there was no vocational training or state examinations in those days, school passed very quickly when I entered the top class at eleven. By the age of twelve I had quite firmly decided to take up dressmaking and face the three years apprenticeship without pay. But then war broke out and my mother was left with the Post Office, and Arthur and Phyllis still at school. Accordingly, when I left school at Easter 1916, I went to work with Amanda Powell, our neighbour, at George Holloway's Steam Sewing Factory at Stroud, which by then had expanded to take in the premises over the Kendrick Street frontage. I didn't see anything of the steam sewing process, but sat at a bench with thirty other girls and sewed buttons on men's trousers *ad infinitum*.

Generally, I was very impressed by the quality and interests of my colleagues, particularly Amanda Powell, who cycled from Randwick with me daily and was a veritable encyclopaedia. She read all the romantic authors, particularly Trollope, as well as Jane Austen and the classics, and we often spent a happy lunch hour in the old library (now the Spiritualist church) with other colleagues, before eating our sandwiches in the church gardens. The pay was piecework and brought in 5s or so per week, but after a year I received the offer of employment by Mr Lee, the Wallbridge outfitter, when he visited the Post Office on deliveries. Most of his men were called up and he needed a travelling saleswoman.

Actually the job, which was at the warehouse adjoining the Stroudwater canal at Wallbridge, now the site of Butt's car park, consisted mostly of packing and book-keeping, but two days a week I scoured the countryside between Stroud and Dursley on my bicycle, with carrier and basket full of boxes containing ladies' and gents' apparel and towels, etc. This was most exhilarating during the summer months, especially when I was joined by Mr Lee's daughter, after she left high school the following year. Our favourite route was from Selsley

George Holloway's main sewing room c.1910.

'ALADDIN'S CAVE' - SPOTS CINEMA IN LANSDOWNE
- & A CHAPLIN PROGRAMME FOR ALL THE FAMILY !

to Dursley along the Cotswold Edge. At Nympsfield, after a long push up Selsley Hill, we would rest to eat sandwiches and admire the view across the Severn Valley to the Welsh mountains. We would then proceed on our rounds, loads becoming gradually lighter, and freewheel down Crawley Hill into Uley. This was a scattered stone village and entailed much walking and pushing up rough tracks to outlying farms. We then cycled the return trip, some fifteen miles in all.

When trade was particularly good, and commission (at sixpence in the pound) permitted, we would cycle the two miles from Uley on into Dursley, board the Dursley Donkey to Stonehouse, and then cycle the three miles back to the warehouse.

Stroud School of Science and Art (built 1899).

Whilst at Lee's, I learned the rudiments of book-keeping, packing and stock-keeping, as well as the art of salesmanship. These were halcyon days for we youngsters, despite my father's absence at the front, and by 1918 Fred was a young man-about-town and Arthur had started an engineering apprenticeship at Lodgemore Mill. In the fashion to get 'up-to-date' he built his first crystal set wireless receiver and, as soon as he could afford it, bought a secondhand BSA motorcycle on which he made many pioneer trips accompanied by his friend and fellow-devotee, Lewis Ballinger of Myrtle Cottage.

Phyllis was a bright schoolgirl and I, to my knowledge, was the first

60

AFTER A 'HARD DAY'S SELL', MISS LEE AND I TAKE A WELL EARNED RIDE ON THE 'DURSLEY DONKEY', — AND CHANGE AT COALEY FOR STONEHOUSE

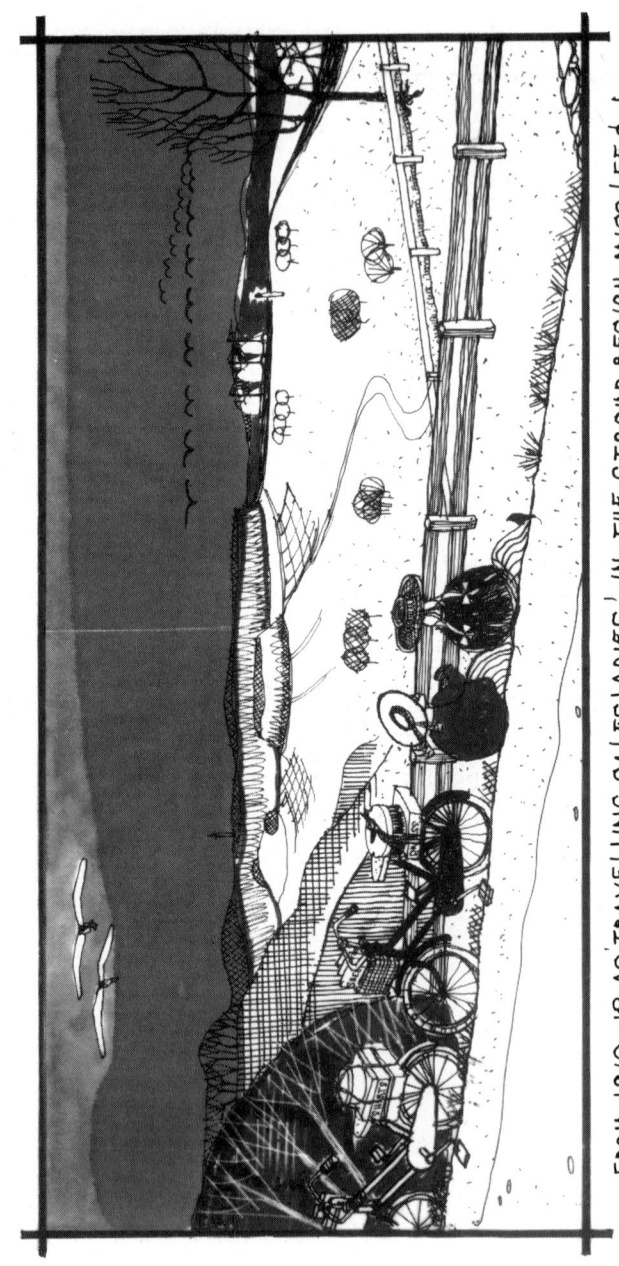

FROM 1916-18 AS 'TRAVELLING SALESLADIES' IN THE STROUD REGION MISS LEE & I
WORKED HARD ON THE DURSLEY RUN' - BUT ALWAYS RESTED AT NYMPSFIELD HILL.

WE ARRIVE AT OUR UNCLE JOSH'S INN AT BERKELEY
— TO BE MET BY HIS PET TORTOISES!

travelling saleswoman in Stroud. We still worked a six-day week, with half-day off on Thursday afternoon, so Arthur and I used to make short cycle trips on Sunday afternoons and more extensive ones on public holidays. These took in places as far apart as Dursley, where Uncle Jess had his shop, to the Whiteway colony at Miserden where we were intrigued to see the communal lifestyle and bohemian dress. Our favourite ride, however, was to Uncle Josh's pub, the George, at Berkeley. This was a good twelve miles each way, and more if we took

UNCLE JESS AND AUNT JANE'S FURNITURE STORE
-UNIVERSAL TROPHIES OF LIFE'S GREAT MYSTERY!

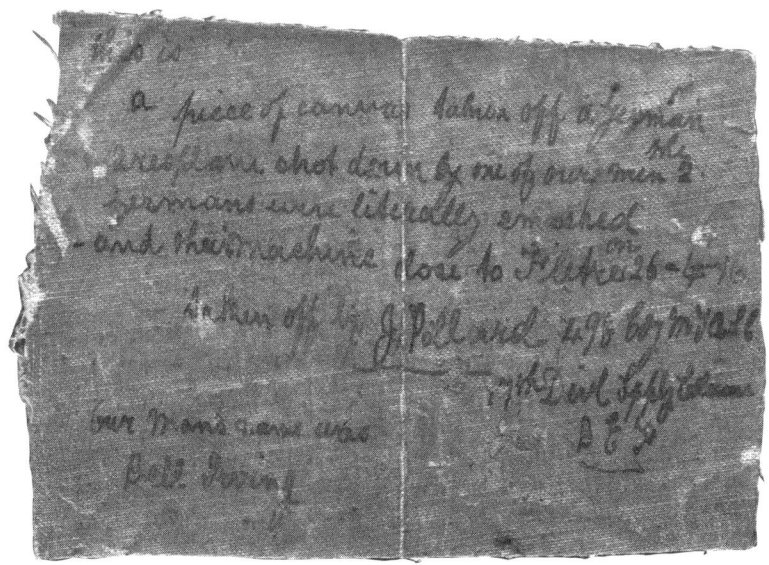

My Father's trophy of 'Bloody April' 1915
(inscribed German aircraft canvass taken at Fletres).

the longer route along the Berkeley canal, to explore the banks of the Severn. We were intrigued by the sailing trows which were still in use in those days – flat-bottomed box-like boats with two lowering masts for canal work and a square top-sail as well as fore-and-aft canvas. We watched the tidal bore and boys fishing for elvers during the Easter migration. We also saw the large basket salmon-weirs in the summer, and watched coracle-fishing, little changed for thousands of years.

My uncle's pub at Berkeley was a tiny Georgian building on the High Street and had a slight nautical flavour, as it was sometimes frequented by sailors from Sharpness Port nearby, where Baltic coasters traded softwood, to be taken by canal to the England's Glory match factory at Gloucester. Uncle Josh and Aunt Fanny had four girls and two boys, and were a happy-go-lucky lot. They kept tortoises, which were always escaping into the road and occasionally run over by carts.

Whilst working in Stroud, I spent two evenings each week at the School of Science and Art, where I studied dress design. Another might be devoted to the exploits of Charlie Chaplin – if I could get Fred to accompany me to 'Spots', which was almost opposite his office. After evening classes, I was often escorted home by Ernie Watkins, a pleasant lad from Paganhill, who was studying commercial subjects. It was at about that time I met a young sailor by the name of Bill Wenman, then serving with the Fifth Light Cruiser Squadron at Harwich, in the Wireless Branch. Bill's family had been bakers at Bampton, Oxfordshire, for generations, but he had been orphaned at eight and sent to the *Arethusa*, where he became stoically independant. I was to correspond with him for several years, both during his period with the Royal Navy, and afterwards when he joined the Merchant Navy. One evening, Bill came to visit me when I arrived home from evening classes with Ernie and a fight ensued, but as my dealings with boys were entirely platonic, peace was soon restored.

One of my most traumatic experiences at this time was the occasion when my brakes failed on Blenheim Hill, due, I now suspect, to lack of maintenance during my father's absence, and I was catapulted through the hedge to land unconscious. Fortunately Amanda Powell was passing at the time and she helped me to Blenheim Cottage for first aid.

My brother Fred was under some pressure from Uncle Jess to join up, as indeed was his ambition at the time. He was, however, a chronic sufferer from bronchitis and failed his first medical at Stroud. Not to be outdone, he re-applied at Gloucester, where the redoubtable uncle was Recruiting Sergeant, and was duly accepted. He joined the Signal Corps, and after a brief training and home leave, was sent to France.

Life was now becoming grimmer as the casualty lists mounted and rationing was introduced, though the latter was of little effect in the country where we grew most of our food. The U-boat attacks were increasing, however, and promised to become critical. Whilst Uncle Jess was at the recruiting office, Aunt Jane was short-handed in the shop, and my mother was persuaded to allow me to assist them at Dursley and live in. Though not particularly enthusiastic to leave my roving commission, I dutifully complied and again boarded the Dursley Donkey.

The Dursley–Coaley line – all 2½ miles of it – was built by the Dursley and Midland Junction Railway in 1856 to serve the mills, and had no less than seven private sidings. It was initially powered by an open cab saddle tank engine purchased from the contractors. In 1883–85 the company, now the Midland Railway, had two Johnson tank engines built at Derby, which actually survived in use until the cessation of passenger traffic in 1962. It drew a single coach on weekdays, and two on Saturdays, but on my Sunday trip home I had to walk to Coaley across the fields.

Aunt Jane was a compulsive 'driver' with a congenital need for constant employment which she tended to communicate to others. She was also considerate and arranged piano and shorthand lessons in the town, for my 'improvement'. I was, however, kept much to myself and

60,000 GAS SHELLS.

Terrific Bombardment Prior To The New German Attack.

A heavy and determined attack was begun against us this morning, a considerable distance north of our recent battles, on about 11 miles front between Armentieres and La Bassee Canal, writes Mr. Philip Gibbs.

This new attack was preceded by a long concentrated bombardment, which gradually increased during the last day or two, until it reached great heights of fury on Monday night and early yesterday morning. The enemy used poison gas in immense quantities, and it may be estimated that during the night he flung over 60,000 gas shells in order to create a wide zone of this evil vapour, and stupefy our gunners, transport, and infantry; if they were caught without their masks.

His gunfire reached to many towns and villages behind the lines like Bethune, Armentieres, Vermelles, Philosophe, Merville, and Estaires, and it did not cease round Armentieres until 11.30 a.m. yesterday, though farther south from Fleurbaix his infantry attack was in progress at eight o'clock, and his barrage lifted in order to let his troops advance. The strength of his attack is not yet known with any certainty, but three divisions are in that area. It is probable that he has other forces engaged.

Part of our line was held by Portuguese troops, who for a long time have been between Laventie and Neuve Chapelle, holding positions which were subject to severe raids from time to time. They are now in the thick of this battle, most fiercely beset, and fighting gallantly.

It is a battle over old and famous ground, where in March, 1915, there was most deadly strife. It is awkward ground for attack, and bad weather for such ground, because the enemy has to advance across dead flat marshes, cut through and through by an intricate system of canals, which must be all flooded now after the heavy rain and shellfire which has broken the banks.

'The indiscriminate use of gas shells by the Germans in a last desperate effort to "break through", following the failure of the main 1918 Spring Offensive on Amiens, killed many men who just didn't happen to be wearing gas masks' (from the Daily Sketch *for Wednesday, April 10th 1918.)*

the company of her young assistant Margaret and missed the social life of the small industrial town. Indeed, the greatest thrill at this time was to catch the Dursley Donkey on Saturday evening to spend Sunday at home. I was thoroughly intrigued by the contents of Uncle's furniture store, which was crammed with the artifacts of diverse cultures, collected during his 'colonial' days.

THE LADS 'SIGN ON' OUTSIDE THE RISING SUN &
THE LASSIES PROVIDE WELCOME ENCOURAGEMENT.

Back at the Post Office there were, of course, all the usual chores to be done, but I was always glad to assist my mother, and at this time we attended Longcourt House after church, to help the ladies sewing and knitting for the lads at the front. I also recall the big recruiting sergeant (*not* my Uncle Jess) who set up his headquarters outside the Rising Sun one summer evening to boost recruitment, with some encouragement from the local lasses. Little did we envisage the horrors of trench warfare at this time.

When April 1918 arrived there seemed some hope of a termination to hostilities, and we were delighted to hear that my brother Fred was to get home leave. This was indeed good news, but very short-lived as some days later my mother received the official telegraph that he had died in a gas-attack near Ypres. She was mortified, especially as she had had such difficulty with his initial survival after the death of her two first-born. . . . *Sic Transit Gloria Mundi*. It never ceases to amaze me that, despite the transitory nature of human experience, Belgian buglers still play the Last Post at Ypres every evening at sunset.

Fred, being some four years older than me, was not perhaps, so close as Arthur, who was two years my junior. If Arthur was the practical

68

THE WARTIME 'KNITTING & SEWING' SESSIONS AT LONGCOURT —
THE OLDER LADIES (CORRECTLY) KEEP THEIR HATS ON!

mechanic, and fairly extrovert, Fred was the philosopher and quietly introvert. As far as I know he hadn't any girlfriends and was usually to be seen out walking or sketching, or indoors with his head in a book. It is difficult to surmise how he would have developed, had he lived. I suppose he would have made a success of his chosen career as a journalist or writer. To 'break through' in those days was difficult from a modest background but, like Arthur, he would doubtless have obtained further education by means of night school or the apprenticeship system.

Soon afterwards, my father was sent to a Bristol hospital as a war invalid, and shortly transferred to Standish hospital nearby. He was in a poor way from general exhaustion and, after a long period of illness, died two years later. He was always totally satisfied with his lot, never bucked 'the system', and firmly believed in resurrection. I duly returned home to comfort my mother. Years later Uncle Jess was able to procure her a small pension.

Randwick's memorial to Great War dead – Walter Brain, Wm. and Ernest Mills, Wm. and Samuel Bennett, Edward Smith, Alfred Pearce, Oliver and Wm. Harmer, Bertram Anderson, Oliver Edmonds, Percy Hill, Fred Pollard, Henry Vick and Samuel Watkins.

DOMESTICITY

From April 1918, when Fred was killed, to May 1921, when my father died, I lived at home, running the Post Office and helping with my father during his illness. Until the pension for my father materialised some years later, my mother managed on a few shillings from the Post Office and a few more from sewing, and occasionally taking in boarders. The latter were usually friends of the vicar and of a quiet academic background. Provided one was fit, kept chickens and grew vegetables, one wasn't too badly off, but it meant that housekeeping had to be conducted as an exact science. A pig's head not only produced brawn but soup, and even the scraps of cloth which brother Arthur was able to procure from the mill were utilized to manufacture hooked rugs. The only problem with the latter was the limited colour range produced by grey suiting, red melton cloth and green baise! We also made bold patchwork counterpanes and cushions, and the whole contrasted nicely with plain white walls and scrubbed floors. Cooking was done on a wood-burning stove, and fires were rarely lit in bedrooms. Lighting was by Aladdin paraffin lamps, and generally much less trying to the eyes than electricity. Medicine was still largely home-made from herbs grown in the garden or collected on the Ash, and old authorities like Mrs Mann were much in demand for advice and prescription. Food was rationed both during and after the war, and this applied to meat, fats and sugar. I still have some unused jam and lard coupons!

During the latter months of 1921, my mother was becoming reasonably adjusted to widowhood, and my sister had left Randwick school to join the Domestic Science School at Gloucester as a boarder. My brother Arthur, at seventeen, was very much the 'man of the house' and I felt that I could look further afield for employment and interest. Reverend Hayward had finally retired after long years of service to the parish, and Reverend Nash was installed. He was a keen sportsman,

71

MINISTRY OF FOOD.

NATIONAL RATION BOOK (B).

INSTRUCTIONS.

Read carefully these instructions and the leaflet which will be sent you with this Book.

1. The person named on the reference leaf as the holder of this ration book must write his name and address in the space below, and must write his name and address, and the serial number (printed upside down on the back cover) in the space provided to the left of each page of coupons.

Food Office of } Issue .... Stroud Rural .... Date .... 21 OCT 19..

Signature of Holder .... Evelyn Pollard

Address .... Post Office, Randwick nr Stroud Glos

2. For convenience of writing at the Food Office the Reference Leaf has been put opposite the back cover, and has (purposely) been printed upside down. It should be carefully examined. If there is any mistake in the entries on the Reference Leaf, the Food Office should be asked to correct it.

3. The holder must register this book at once by getting his retailers for butcher's meat, bacon, butter and margarine, sugar and tea respectively, to write their names and the addresses of their shops in the proper space on the back cover. Previous retailers in boarding houses, hostels, schools, and similar establishments should not register their books until they leave the establishment.

4. The ration book may be used only by or on behalf of the holder, to buy rationed food for him, or members of the same household, or guests sharing common meals. It may not be used to buy unrationed food nor any other rations.

M 33 (New)

(Continued see next page.)

IF FOUND, RETURN TO ANY FOOD OFFICE

NAMES OF RETAILERS.

Name and Address of BUTCHER.

W Berns Randwick

Name and Address of BACON Retailer.

Name & Address of BUTTER & MARGARINE Retailer.

Name and Address of LARD Retailer.

Name and Address of SUGAR Retailer.

Name and Address of TEA Retailer.

Name and Address of Retailer for

Name and Address of Retailer for

J 10

Nº 226388

captained the cricket team, and got on well with the youth of the village. Living next door to the vicarage, I assisted Mrs Nash in many ways, and when her husband became curate to the Harrow mission at Latimer Road, Shepherds Bush during the summer of 1921, I was invited to take a post as nanny to the young son of his vicar, Revd Carnegie. This was the challenge that I needed, and I gladly accepted.

I never regretted my three years of domesticity with my mother at the Post Office. She was good company, an excellent manager and, like Queen Mary, she never made a public speech – and never needed to. I took a good look at our fourteenth-century church tower and humped my modest luggage to Stroud station, bound for the great metropolis.

PART III
METROPOLIS
AND
MARRIAGE

Mother and I in 1922.

'NANNY'
POLLARD

After a brisk trip by train and underground, I arrived at the Harrow mission in some trepidation, but was immediately reassured by the kindness of Revd and Mrs Carnegie. I was allocated a room adjoining the two nurseries on the top floor, and introduced to Mr and Mrs Bond, the butler and housekeeper, who were the only staff to live in and occupied the lower ground floor accommodation. I also met my new charge, six months old Master David.

To my surprise, I wasn't expected to wear uniform and could eat in my own room, except on social occasions when I dined with the family. At the same time, I could nip down the back stairs to have supper with the Bonds, an amenable older couple, if I wished. I was encouraged to use the back garden, which adjoined the parishoners' day nursery and had easy access to the shops and parks of the West End. Master David, though young when I arrived, was well-behaved and intelligent, and I was to have home leave twice a year.

I soon settled into the friendly and relaxed atmosphere, but found the Metropolis somewhat daunting initially. Because of congenital short-sightedness, previously undetected, I just couldn't identify the buses. Mrs Carnegie heard about this, probably from Mr Bond, and promptly sent me to an optician, where I was duly fitted out with pince-nez. I could now not only see properly for the first time, but improved my 'governess image' enormously. My employers never once attempted to influence my judgement either personally or professionally and, indeed, the whole of my four years service with them was totally fulfilling.

Although 'the Scrubs' was not all elegance, the influence of George III and his Architect, Henry Holland, was still considerable. The advent of the electric lift had not yet caused the disruption of the London skyline which was to come, and the walk-up height practicable for domestic buildings was still five storeys. By means of careful route planning, one could push a pram upon a succession of grassed or

Master David Carnegie and 'Nanny' – on the beach at Bridport in 1923.

tree-lined areas as far as the 'classy' shops of Kensington High Street. Needless to say, my country dark and light grey costumes were soon augmented with a smart new navy blue one which I obtained at a local sale for £1.

My daily routine, as I recall, was as follows for weekdays:

8.30 a.m.	Breakfast with David
9.30 a.m.	Walk pram through Holland Park, etc.
11.00 a.m.	Home and rest for David, when I did sewing
1.00 p.m.	Lunch with family
2.00 p.m.	Walk pram on Scrubs, etc.
4.00 p.m.	Tea in Day Nursery. Read to David. Mostly books by Beatrix Potter, which were then appearing, or improvise stories
5.00 p.m.	David joins parents
6.00 p.m.	David's bath and bedtime and my free period
7.00 p.m.	Supper with the Bonds

Sundays didn't vary much, except for attendance at morning service.

Mrs Nash advised me on tours to make around London, including exhibitions of note, and Mr Bond made a point of showing me the sights

BEING SHORTSIGHTED I COULDN'T READ THE BUS NAMES
—UNTIL THE CARNEGIES KINDLY PROVIDED SPECTACLES

of the city. After a short while I was also introduced by my Aunt Jane to a friend of hers from her nursing days in India, a Mrs Matthews, who lived with her husband and five children in Camden Town. He was a 'pukka' Indian Army Cavalryman, complete with spurs, and I enjoyed the occasional visit to the theatre with his elder children Kathleen and Frank. The latter emigrated to Australia when he was twenty-one, but I continued to visit and help Kathleen and her mother with the sewing.

Revd and Mrs Carnegie regularly took holidays with friends and relations, leaving Revd Nash in charge of church duties for two to three

79

I HANG ON GRIMLY & PULL WHILST 'DERBY' DIGS H/S HEELS IN PRIOR TO
DASHING OFF AT BREAKNECK SPEED — AND RUNNING ME DOWN!

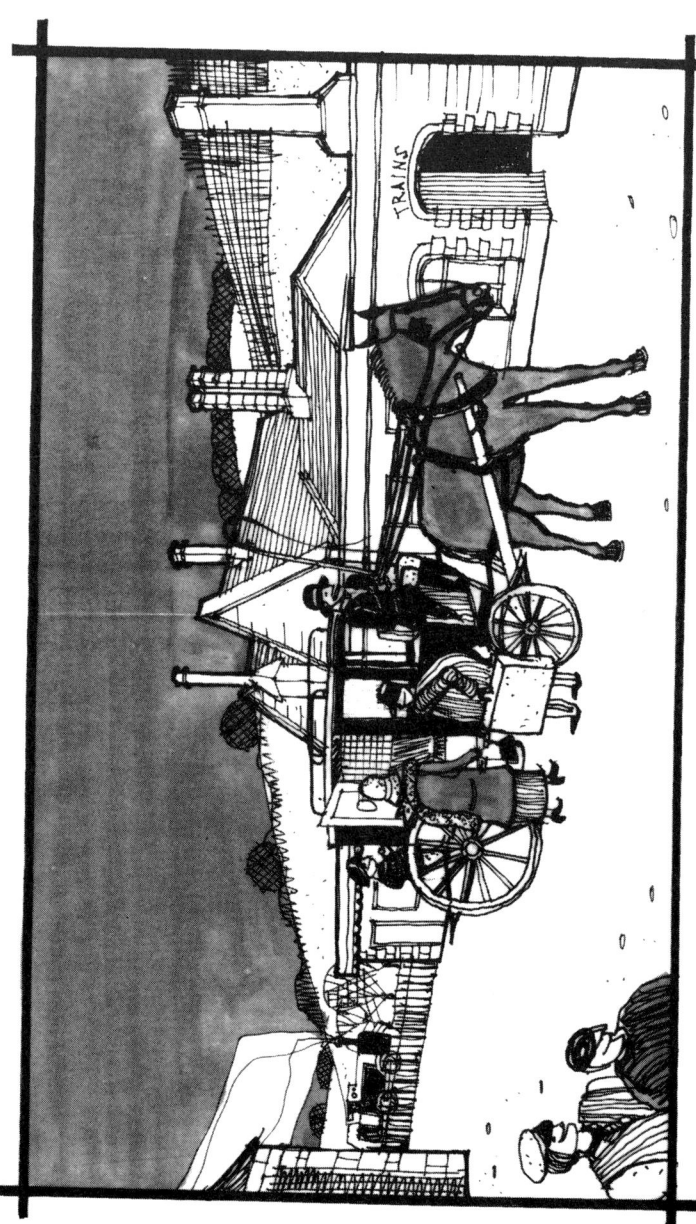

I BOARD HARKERS HEARSE OUTSIDE STROUD STATION & THE BOYS SHOUT
"WHIP BEHIND GOV'NER" — TO DISCOURAGE NON-PAYING PASSENGERS

weeks. On these occasions I dined *en famille* with our hosts. My favourite summer visit was to Revd Carnegie's sister at Grendon, Warwickshire, where her husband, Revd Crawley-Boevey, was vicar. They had two small daughters and one son, the indoor staff consisting of a governess, cook and parlourmaid. As these three girls were sisters and hailed from Gloucester, we got on famously. The Crawley-Boeveys also hailed from Gloucestershire, where the family held a Baronetcy at Flaxley Abbey for generations.

The great event at Grendon, other than delightful country walks, was the Donkey Derby. The children, who had many pet animals, would harness their donkey to the governess cart, which we then attempted to drive to Atherstone, the nearest town. Needless to say, the spoiled creature went very grudgingly, until he was pointed homewards, when he would set off at a gallop and land us in the ditch! We also visited Lady Scott, Mrs Carnegie's aunt, at Ramsgate, though this was generally a somewhat more formal occasion. Of the house visitors at the mission, I chiefly recall Mr Longman, the well-known publisher, who was most genial.

I made most of my clothes at this time and, my wages being paid monthly, I was able to save quite a nice sum. Amongst other luxuries, I bought high heeled shoes and a 'fox' fur. However, it was pleasant to get back to the country for leave and freedom from routine. On several occasions I ran into Ernie Watkins and had a pleasant chat, and I continued to correspond with Bill Wenman from time to time, who was then working in America.

Looking back, it is amazing how quickly the time passed during my four years at the mission. I saw the sights of London, including that last great Carnival of Empire, the Wembley Exhibition of 1924, and no sooner had Master David reached school age than conditions at home suggested my return. Though it is true that Nanny should never supplant Mother in a child's affection, David was very sad at my leaving, and so was I.

THE WANDERINGS

OF

WILLIAM WENMAN, MARINER

Despite Bill Wenman's desire to travel, the Wenman family had been firmly 'land-based' in the Witney area since Richard Wenman, woolstapler of Calais, was buried in the parish church in AD 1500.

From the senior branch, his descendant Richard Wenman was knighted by Essex after the Cadiz raid in 1596, and providently purchased an Irish Viscountcy in 1628, which survived until 1800. In the junior branches, a series of large families turned yeoman farmers to journeymen, until William's great-grandfather Thomas was able to set up his bakery at Bampton in 1826, after apprenticeship in Abingdon, where he married Hannah Embury in 1819. They had seven children and his second son, John, took over the bakery on Thomas's death, extended it to Northleach and duly passed it to Bill's father, John Francis.

John Francis had six children by his first marriage to Polly Taylor who died after childbirth in 1894. He married Esther Smith in 1897 and had five more children, of which Bill was the third. Unfortunately, John Francis died in 1908, leaving the younger children wards of the parish, under the supervision of an uncle, John Young.

In January 1916, when he was fourteen, Bill, together with his younger brothers Embrey and Henry, were sent to the *Arethusa* training ship at Greenhithe, Kent, whilst their elder brother Arthur joined the British Expeditionary Force in France. The *Arethusa* ran a tough regime in those days, beginning with scaling the masts at 6.30 a.m. and holy-stoning the deck before breakfast, but it instilled a stoic self-sufficiency.

Whilst in training at Billericay, Essex, around midnight on 23rd September 1916, he witnessed the destruction of the German airship L32 by our recently-established night-fighters, armed with explosive bullets. During this period of multi-Zeppelin raids, the lads were taken

AIRSHIPS LEADER KAPITAN PETER STRASSER REPEATS
"POOR PETERSON" AS L32 PLUNGES IN FLAMES & L33
CRASH LANDS – LT. MATHY IMPASSIVELY REQUESTS ORDERS

out into the fields, away from target buildings. As they lay amongst the turnips on this occasion, they became aware of a tiny flicker of light moving at high altitude. This gradually developed into a fireball as successive gas-bags were ignited along the ship's length. It landed, a blazing inferno, in a field at Snail's Farm nearby, several of the crewmen jumping to their deaths. The German dead were duly buried in the local churchyard with full military honours, and all involved attended, including Lieutenant John Sowrey, the pilot who fired the fatal incendiary shots. The five smaller airships which raided the east coast returned successfully and did little damage.

We are told that Luftschiffsführer Peter Strasser, who observed the holocaust from the control car of the L31 nearby, was appalled by the fate of his protegé Kapitan Peterson and crewmen. Nevertheless, despite the loss of two of his best ships, the L32 and the L33 (which was forced down near West Mersea and its crew captured after successfully bombing London), Strasser continued to lead raids at higher and higher altitudes, until he was finally brought down on the 5th August 1918, leading a five-Zeppelin raid in the L70.

After war service as boy telegraphist on the destroyer *Dauntless*, during which time he 'stood by' at Jutland, Bill joined the Merchant

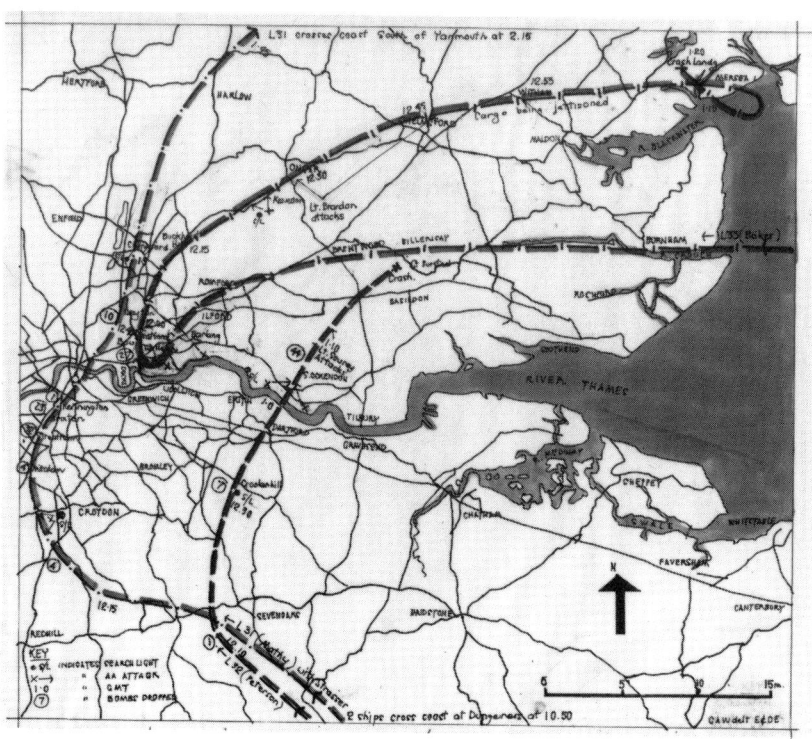

A well planned three-pronged airship attack on the 23rd and 24th September 1916 foiled by ack-ack and night fighters.

Navy and made several trips to America and the Near East. It is difficult to appreciate that, on tramp steamers at this time, crew were still automatically signed on for two years, travelled anywhere in the world at the company's desire, and did not even know where they would go next, until they arrived in port, unloaded, and found a fresh cargo, or received telegraphed orders from the company. Cargoes could be anything from coal to grain and the holds were thoroughly washed before reloading. Steam coal for fuel also had to be hand loaded. The most dangerous cargo was probably timber as, though not strictly overloaded, deck cargoes were carried for economy and in rough weather these could shift and cause a capsize.

Messing was personal and crewmen had to cook their own food, and *provide* it on short runs, or go hungry. Most skippers still worked 'watch by watch' – four hours on and four off, round the clock – and as

The 'old' Arethusa, *which Bill Wenman joined at thirteen before becoming a naval boy telegraphist.*

SS Tregangle, *world 'tramp' on which Ernie and Bill served with a mostly Norwegian crew – coming into Rotterdam, 28 September 1923.*

crew still had to eat, sleep at sea was rare. In bad weather, or if cargo shifted, skippers would keep both watches on deck. Crew provided their own mattress, the traditional 'donkey's breakfast', which was conveniently burnt when in port as the forecastle was invariably flea-ridden.

The temptation to jump ship was great and, after a particularly unpleasant run, Bill and his young Scots friend decided to stay ashore in America – during the time that I was in London. They spent the first night in an American gaol! Following negotiations with the Consul, they tried house-painting, smuggling (during prohibition), and once even begged from the Newport–Norfolk Virginia ferry queue. Once they enlisted aboard an east coast schooner, only to be put ashore at Rio after the captain discovered that they knew nothing about sail, and couldn't tell a sheet from a brace or a halliard. They then tried the east coast barge traffic, where a small tug would haul three large barges for economy. During rough weather the barges were let out on long hawsers (with one helmsman apiece) to avoid collision, so the job proved a somewhat lonely one.

After two years in America, Bill and his Scots friend had many adventures. On one occasion they were put ashore for broaching cargo – a crime of which they definitely were not guilty, and on another occasion were blown up and seriously burned when a cargo of slack coal developed fire damp and they entered a companion-way whilst smoking. The classic incident, however, occurred soon after the Russian Revolution, when they were put ashore in Leningrad with a Scandinavian crew by a skipper who despaired of the Norwegians' 'Bolshi' attitude. They were duly issued with meal and cinema tickets by local Party Officials and, being realists, took great care to observe all the required social conventions, such as wearing party stickers and standing with the populace in the Red Square and singing the *Internationale* with gusto. Their diligence was duly appreciated as, before long, they were put on a German boat (with a Socialist skipper), by which means they finally reached home.

Bill had had enough of wandering and decided to contact me again when he was on the *Tegantee* doing the Amsterdam–New York run with a Scandinavian crew. The skipper would 'hit the bottle' once out of port, and leave command to the first mate – who fortunately was an excellent navigator and, before the days of gyro-compasses and radar fixes, would bring the ship, by dead reckoning alone, bang onto the Statue of Liberty after 3000 miles!

During his latter years at sea, Bill's great friend and mentor was Ernie Daniels, an old sail man of great experience, who had once sailed on the *Terra Nova*, before Captain Scott took her over. They continued to keep

ERNIE DANIELS AND SEAGOING COMPANIONS CHECK THE
WIND DIRECTION & SAIL 'SET' ON A PASSING TROW

in touch for many years after leaving the sea and Ernie had taken a tiny
whitewashed cottage at Saul on the Severn, which he also called 'Terra
Nova'. He was then a widower and kept his living-room full of ship's
gear, charts and memorabilia. He continued to live as if he were at sea,
observing watch times and nautical conventions. When parting he
would always give his navigational 'fix', and say 'Don't forget to report
me to Lloyds, Bill'.

WANDERER'S RETURN

During Summer 1924, I sadly decided to leave London, though the only unpleasant thing about the situation was the occasional London smogs. David was reaching school age and could be placed in the local nursery school, and my mother was worried about Phyllis, who felt unfulfilled at home, but was not yet ready to face independant employment. Whilst on home leave, we all discussed the matter and decided that my sister and I should take a joint post in service locally – if we could find one.

We duly presented ourselves at numerous domestic agencies in Stroud and, as several weeks passed without success as a cook/nanny team, we decided to accept a joint position as cook/parlourmaid with Lady Baker, of the Grove, Stonehouse. This was a large house, in spacious grounds, with a somewhat monastic atmosphere. Lady Baker was lately returned from India and lived with her son who administered the estate. The staff were Miss Taylor, an elderly housekeeper, and one gardener, as well as my sister and I.

We settled in quickly and I took over the cooking, to gain experience. At this time Mr Baker was set on chicken farming and the kitchen was often crammed with incubating chicks. Time passed pleasantly, Phyllis gained confidence, and we spent many happy hours walking over Doverow Hill to Randwick on our half-days off. I was twenty-three, and still unattached. But not for long as, one fine day when I was in the midst of 'incubation' duties, who should appear at the trades entrance, but my wandering mariner, complete with stetson, yellow waistcoat and bellbottoms – carrying a live parrot and a stuffed alligator. The *Tegantee* had finally docked at Amsterdam and he was staying with his sister at Stonehouse. Mr Baker was musically inclined and played the piano, whilst his fiancée was a violinist. I shall always remember their romantic strains floating across the lawn at the Grove that evening.

My friendship with Bill prospered and we became engaged during

THE WANDERER'S RETURN

the late summer of 1924. He transferred to Elder and Ffyfes line, as quartermaster on the *Bayano*, sailing regularly at five-week intervals from Avonmouth with general cargo to Kingston, Jamaica, and returning with green bananas, complete with tarantula spiders – so he now visited me regularly.

My sister too, overcoming her shyness, was keeping company with a quiet, romantic young man called Fred Barnett, who lived at Whiteshill, but attended church at Randwick. He was dedicated to modern technology, but was equally at home in the backwoods.

90

AT TRINIDAD THE CABIN BOY IS INCREDULOUS
—"WHY YO' LOOK AT ME LIKE DAT — YO' LIL DUCKY
CHILE — MAMMY GARDNER WON' EAT YOU" —

92

DOUBLE
HARNESS

W hen 1925 arrived, Bill and I decided to marry. Unemployment was around the two million mark and property difficult to obtain, so, with my mother's complete approval, we decided to live at the Post Office initially, as Bill would only be home for a few days every five weeks. Everything was arranged and we were married by Revd Moore at St John's, Randwick on 22nd July.

Wedding group, 22 July 1925.

The wedding attire for myself and my bridesmaids (sister Phyllis and sister-in-law Emily) was entirely home-made, my dress consisting of white ankle-length crêpe de chine, with floating side panels, long full sleeves and tulle veil. The bridesmaids had similar dresses in blue crêpe with wired Flemish bonnets to match. About fifty guests attended.

Phyllis stayed on at the Grove and persuaded a friend of hers from the Forest of Dean to take my place. They had been at cookery school together and got on well. Later that year Bill was offered a post as Steward at the Seamen's Rest, Bristol, and in order to get him settled ashore, we accepted a joint appointment. During the general strike of 1926, Bill saw an advertisement requiring unskilled men to train as drivers on goods trains. Pay was good, he was not politically concerned, and permanent jobs were promised in the long term. He applied and was duly accepted, so we sought, and found, rooms close to Cabot's Tower. This was not a particularly happy move from my viewpoint, as he seldom got home through the picket lines at night, and at the end of the strike men were reinstated and no new jobs were immediately available. However, we returned to mother for a while and applied for a joint post in service with General Sir Henry Stanton at Bourton-on-the-Water. We were gratified when Lady Stanton appeared at the Post Office to interview us personally, during a visit to her husband's relatives at Paganhill House nearby. She engaged us immediately and we took up residence at their Bourton home, a Cotswold manor-house called Burghfields, bearing the General's family arms and motto, *Dum Spiro Spero*. As well as Bill and myself, who functioned as butler/cook, they kept a young parlour-maid living in and a gardener called Norris, who lived at the gate-lodge. Their daughter lived at home.

'MRS. MCNAB' TELLS A JOKE AT THE GENERAL'S DINNER
+ HER HUSBAND LOOKS GLUM - THE STAFF ARE 'IN FITS'.

BILL DOES A PUSH START & ! A RESTRICTED TROT READY TO DIVE FOR THE PILLION AS MR. NORRIS STANDS BY ! AT THE GATEHOUSE — AND THE SWANS LOOK WARY !

Considering the quietness of the district at that time, they did a lot of entertaining, especially dinner parties. Mrs Cook from the village helped on these occasions, and Bill became a good butler, except for a certain inability to keep a straight face when guests told a good joke! And there was plenty of humour, especially as her Ladyship's brother was a pleasant young man called Wilfred Hyde-White.

At this juncture, my husband bought a second-hand motorbike, a Beardmore Precision which, with luck, took us home on Sunday afternoons. Having no clutch or throttle, it needed a push start up the drive, during which I staggered behind in my fashionable hobble skirt and cloche hat, ready to dive for the pillion as the engine sputtered into life. Mr Norris waited sceptically at the gatehouse to render first aid as necessary, or fish us out of the river Windrush opposite if we overshot. The machine had a leather belt drive, known as the 'bootlace', which seemed endlessly expandable until it would unexpectedly jump off the rear wheel-rim and coil viciously around my legs like a boa constrictor.

On one hot, sultry, Sunday afternoon in the summer of 1927, we set off, having duly cooked and served lunch and prepared an extensive cold buffet supper, to drive the seventy miles to Randwick and back by 'lights out'. After the usual series of teething troubles common to mechanical vehicles in those days, and following the standard routine of dismounting and pushing the heavy machine up hills, we finally broke down near the garage at Northleach crossroads. No-one was available for repairs on Sunday so, not to be done out of our half-day's leave, we left the bike at the garage and trudged the ten miles into Cirencester. The hot, dusty, white stone road glared up at us and we finally arrived at Cirencester station with just enough money to board the Stroud train – and walked a further three miles at the other end. Not to fail our kindly employers, my brother Arthur was good enough to lend us his own machine, a newer and lighter BSA model, and we were relieved to arrive back at Burghfields in good time for 'lights out'.

The General, now retired, was a keen bee-keeper and exhibited honey in local shows. One day he decided to enter a competition for beeswax and demonstrated the procedure for preparation, then left me to boil the wax in a large pan on the kitchen range. Imagine my surprise when the room became full of angry bees seeking their lost wax! I needn't have worried as the General, totally unflustered, returned, complete with hat and mask, and removed the offending pot to the garden. Next day I reheated the wax and strained off the dead bees and, I am relieved to say, the General won first prize.

This was a very happy situation and I was very sorry when my husband, not yet settled from his travels, felt the need to move on. It seems sad to me that the whole Burghfields property has since been

A SWARM OF ANGRY BEES IN THE KITCHEN & GENERAL SIR HENRY STANTON PERFORMS A DASHING RESCUE FOR COOK!

destroyed to build council houses, but such is the march of progress. The tiny limestone gatehouse (from which Mr Norris had to exit to swing on his Norfolk jacket) is, alas, now replaced by an arched entry of truly imperial grandeur – to overscaled houses of machine-made bricks. What a pity that beauty, like happiness, so often passes unnoticed.

Shortly after the saga of the bees, a move was dictated when I found myself pregnant. Bill obtained a regular post as porter at Standish hospital, and we duly returned to the Post Office, where we settled down and awaited the birth.

On 5th November 1927, my sister Phyllis was married to Fred Barnett and, as Revd Moore was still vicar, he gamely suggested that, as it was Guy Fawkes night, we might celebrate the occasion with fireworks on the vicarage lawn. A good time was had by all from both Randwick and Whiteshill villages, though I was forced to watch from the upstairs window on account of my advanced pregnancy.

On 21st February 1928, my son Graham was born in the presence of the newly appointed district nurse, Flora Bennett having by now gracefully relinquished this duty, and my sister's first child, Joyce, was born the following year. To complete the hat trick my brother Arthur shortly afterwards announced his marriage to Evelyn Cann of Drybrook in the Forest of Dean, whom he met at Standish hospital where she was then cook to Dr Dickson. They were duly married at Drybrook early in 1929 and their daughter, Mary, was born the following December.

In the event this was opportune, as my husband was at this time offered a better post at Milford hospital, near Godalming, Surrey, then newly completed as a tuberculosis sanitorium, when Miss Hall, of Standish hospital, was appointed to the matronship. This allowed Evelyn, my new sister-in-law, to assume the duties of the Post Office, enabling my mother to take a well-earned rest. We all benefitted from the changes in our respective ways, but family ties were strong and in 1934 Arthur and Evelyn were to join us at Milford when he, now fully qualified, obtained the post of Deputy Engineer.

But that is another story. For the present, I leave you with the illustration of my first-born peering out of the rear window of the newly established Randwick motor-bus. It has stalled at Vicarage Rise, and all able-bodied men have dismounted to push the struggling vehicle up to the terminus at the war memorial.

'ALL HANDS' PUSH THE NEW MOTORBUS UP POOL RISE
— & 'PRINCE' PLODS BEHIND TO LIGHTEN THE LOAD.

AFTERTHOUGHT

For a modest hill village, the buildings of Randwick were surprisingly good up to the period of the Great War. To my mind, with the possible exception of the council houses, they have been pretty poor since, despite the application of planning law and a plethora of building byelaws. One cannot legislate for delight.

The Iron Age tumuli and defence ditch upon the Ash provide evidence of a firmly established settlement during the second millenia BC whilst the fourteenth-century church tower and cruck cottages at 1–4 Church Street substantiate its medieval pedigree. The church was sensibly enlarged during the eighteenth and nineteenth centuries and boasts several eighteenth-century tablets and brasses to local clothiers, as well as substantial table-tombs in the churchyard. The vicarage is an effective Victorian Gothic building of 1844.

More Hall Manor, of late-Elizabethan times, is a striking transitional renaissance building, with superb stone rainwater spouts, mullioned windows and gable finials, sensitively remodelled in the 1920s, and recently sympathetically extended.

The manor houses of Longcourt, the Rylands, and Blenheim House are well proportioned and beautifully executed in local stone and exhibit a virile mix of classical and romantic features – pointed windows, for instance, at Blenheim house – and date mostly from the Georgian period. The village cottages before 1900 are always appropriate in scale and materials and relate to natural contours.

Cashes Green, at least, has retained a bricky integrity and Townsend, except for a few re-roofings in red tile, is fairly intact.